NLP

How to Analyze People, Use Powerful Communication, and Understand Behavioral Psychology to Win in Business and Relationships

Robert Sanders J.

inattention or otherwise, by any usage or abuse of any policies, processes, or directions contained within is the solitary and utter responsibility of the recipient reader. Under no circumstances will any legal responsibility or blame be held against the publisher for any reparation, damages, or monetary loss due to the information herein, either directly or indirectly.

Respective authors own all copyrights not held by the publisher.

The information herein is offered for informational purposes solely and is universal as so. The presentation of the information is without a contract or any type of guarantee assurance.

The trademarks that are used are without any consent, and the publication of the trademark is without permission or backing by the trademark owner. All trademarks and brands within this book are for clarifying purposes only and are owned by the owners themselves, not affiliated with this document.

DISCLAIMER

With all efforts towards this book, all the
information therein are for educational purposes.
Every achievement has been made to make this
book as complete and accurate as possible. Also,
this book provides information that is up to
releasing date. Therefore, this book should be used
as a guide - not as the ultimate source.

INTRODUCTION

Neuro-linguistic programming (NLP) is the study of mental patterns. This gives you an idea of the mental process used to encode information, the way of thinking and acting.

Neuro-linguistic programming means that our thoughts are composed of words and languages (linguistics), which modify the words that surround us and create programs through neurons. If you repeat certain words frequently, this message becomes a program. These installed programs generate emotions that guide our actions and reactions.

This means that we have installed hundreds of programs throughout our lives even before birth. At the beginning of our life, the program was installed by parents, grandparents, and parent relatives. Then by teachers, friends and media, we accept without acknowledging whether these programs support or harm us. There are also programs we installed ourselves. Similarly, some are good and some are not.

NLP allows people to recognize their programs and those of others more clearly. I remember when I was a child I was given a snack with sweet bread, coffee and milk, which became a habit and then a program. Instead, I was given a ham and cheese snack and a glass of milk as a child, so it became a habit and a program.

In this example, you can see that each has a different program and does not conflict with each other. These programs have been modified or canceled over time if we find that they are no longer functioning in our lives. Neuro-linguistic Programming helps you better understand what programs you have under your belt. It also helps to free yourself from those who are no longer useful for making changes.

NLP makes our language more conscious because it affects our body's biochemistry (see the article "The Importance of Claimed Language"). Saying "how handsome" (feels better) is not the same: "How stupid" (feels worse). And if anyone else says me good or bad, there are biochemical reactions that affect me. Thus, words that pass through neurons in addition to writing a program elicit a response.

Therefore, NLP meets you, optimizes abilities, improves family and work relationships, better controls emotions, changes behavior, stops prosecuting neighbors, and is more positive for your own good. Have thoughts and suggest taking care of your health, realize more positive internal dialogue, have a positive effect on you, keep your balance longer, gain self-knowledge, Earn many benefits.

The most important thing about Neurolinguistics Programming is to find new options in your life and gain the ability to create new spirits. If you do this, you get out of a stalemate and staying in the same does not work. Changing the strategy is important for achieving different results.

Make permanent internal changes by implementing NLP techniques. And if you know how your mind works, you can start telling it, not pointing to a negative program you have installed. The goal is to learn to have better areas of self, emotions and reactions. Neurolinguistics programming allows you to practice selection and staging techniques.

CHAPTER 1
WHAT IS NLP

NLP is a meta- model because it goes beyond simple communication. This meta-model adopts as one of its strategies, key questions to find out what words mean to people. It focuses on the structure of the experience, rather than the content of it. It is presented as the study of the "how" of each person's experiences, the study of the subjective world of people and the ways in which subjective experience is structured and communicated to others, through language.

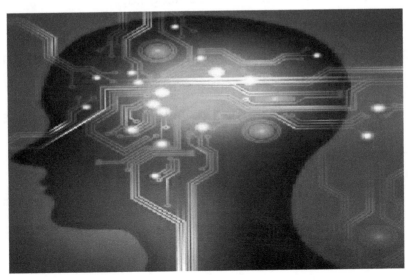

It is a model of communication, a model of behavior, which seeks to describe and systematize a few subtle aspects of communication and somehow contribute to the occurrence of some required result.

NLP studies how people communicate with each other and how they communicate with themselves to use their resources in an optimal way to create certain behavioral alternatives and to obtain certain results.

This allows the behavior to be conceived as a consequence or result of complex neurophysiological processing of the information perceived by the sensory organs. Processes that are represented ordered and systematized in models and strategies,
through communication systems
such as language. These systems have components that make the experience possible and can be intentionally organized and programmed to achieve certain purposes.

Three aspects with respect to the term NLP:

- Programming : refers to the process of organizing the elements of a system (sensory representations), to achieve specific results. Defines the ability to produce and apply behavioral programs . It refers to a mental organization , how mental categories are organized, which serve to interpret the outside world.

- Neuro : (from the Greek Neuron, which means nerve), refers to the sensory perceptions that determine the inner state , both from the neurological and subjective points of view. It represents the basic principle that all behavior is the result of neurological processes .

- Linguistics: (from Latin Lingua, which means language), indicates that the nervous processes are represented and organized sequentially in models and strategies through the system of language and communication. It refers to the means of human communication. It is verbal and nonverbal communication , which is observed in external behavior, which they express when communicating.

Programming refers to organize sensory representations in order to achieve specific results, it represents neurological outcomes in order to achieve improvement in behavior and represents a feature that

13

is not common in all species and forms of communication, which organized sequentially in models and strategies they can improve nervous systems.

From the perspective of NLP, it is this intersection that produces effective and ineffective behaviors, and is responsible for the process behind excellence and human pathology. Many of these patterns were derived from the observation of patterns of excellence of experts in various fields of human communication, including: psychotherapy, administration , hypnosis, law and education

The concept NLP was created by Richard Bandler and Grinder Jonh at the beginning of the seventies. In this regard, the opinion of Bandler which states:

"Neuro- Linguistic programming is the name I invented to avoid the specialization of one field or another ... one of the ways that (NLP) represents, is to focus on human learning ... basically we develop ways to teach people to use your own head. "

Robbins (1991), also provides a significant concept about NLP by considering that it is the study of how language, both verbal and nonverbal, affects the nervous system, that is, that through the process of communication can be directed the brain to achieve optimal results.

It could therefore be said that NLP is a set of tools , procedures , skills and strategies that are very useful in any situation of human interaction . Hence, its usefulness in various fields NLP is a study of human excellence, since it gives the opportunity to continually grow in the emotional, psychological, intellectual , artistic and social aspects and at the same time contributes positively to the progress of others.

These aspects have a high value in the educational field, because that is where the idea of using NLP as a strategic tool for the effectiveness of the teaching - learning process starts.

Thus, it is very probable that the proper application of a communication model such as NLP, helps that professional to increase his communicative power and his persuasive potential in contact with the people around him and, consequently, to increase his effectiveness in their respective role.

NLP is a behavioral science that includes:

- An Epistemology - A system of knowledge and values.
- A Methodology - Processes and procedures to apply knowledge and values.
- Technology - Tools to help the application of knowledge and values.

BACKGROUND OF NEUROLINGUISTIC PROGRAMMING

In the mid-twentieth century, very prominent scientists, including a Russian named Luria, resumed the evidence of the relations between the brain and language accumulated approximately one hundred years ago and asked again how this organ generated what is considered more distinctive of man (thoughts, actions , emotions).

The psychology had devoted his attention to the processes of abnormal behavior and how to achieve lead normal subjects studied. This strategy was in effect until the NLP study began.

NLP was born at the initiative of John Grinder (Psycholinguist) and Richard Bandler (Mathematician,

Psychotherapist, Gestaltist) in the early 1970s, gaining adherents and practical applicability in business, family and personal life . They consider that all effective communication has constants, which, defined systematically, can be learned by those who do not.

The task of both was oriented in search of why some therapists were successful in their treatments. They chose Milton Erickson, Virginia Satir, Fritz Perls and Carls Rogers and identified the behavioral patterns employed by them, the way they performed the verbal inventions, the tone and timbre of their voice, their nonverbal attitudes , their actions, movements and postures among others.

Through the observation study, they found that these therapists had in common a structure or mode of interaction, which allowed them access to a series of powerful communication models to establish some useful rules or guidelines to achieve the goal in different areas of work , within them the educational field.

In this way, when studying the behavior patterns, the language, the illusions of human beings as opposed to those who have no language, they were creating processes, forms of influence, sometimes passing from the unconscious to the conscious the various behaviors obtaining results very important for the understanding of success, failures, sadness, demotivation, changes, stress , etc.

They noticed that with their words and behaviors they produced magical changes in the minds and emotions of the subjects. Then Grinder found verbal patterns that were repeated systematically in these magicians when it came to producing their magic and Bandler found non-verbal patterns that were also repeated systematically. Bandler and Grinder found the structure of that magic that produced the priests. What was previously relegated with the label of Don Natural could now be learned and used.

The initial objectives of NLP have been to exceptional model skills of certain people and help transfer them to others.

The NLP, debate between theoretical models that promote research, is supported by the scientific method , which is the guarantee that new explanations give new definitions, ensuring their legitimacy .

CHARACTERISTICS OF NEUROLINGUISTIC PROGRAMMING

NLP is a pragmatic school of thought , with tools to develop strategic and systematic thinking. It improves the deficiencies and basic principles of what human beings are and to make more flexible behaviors that allow achieving the proposed goals efficiently.

NLP can be characterized:

- NLP has the ability to help human beings grow, resulting in a better quality of life.
- It presents a practical and powerful approach to achieve personal changes because it has a series of techniques that are associated with each other to achieve the behavior that you want to acquire.
- It is conceived as a powerful tool for communication, influence and persuasion, since, through the communication process, the brain can be directed to achieve optimal results.
- It is essentially modeling. The specialists who developed the NLP studied those who were doing things in an excellent way, found their formula and provided the means to repeat the experience.

NLP studies in depth the way in which the brain works, as well as the way in which emotions are constructed and how they affect the individual physically and intellectually. It also proposes a series of techniques (based mainly on creative visualization) that allow increasing self-esteem and self-confidence.

Train for self-regulation by early detection of triggers of unwanted emotional states and offers techniques that allow you to develop your own resources for use in any sensitive emotional situation.

For the development of self-motivation, NLP suggests an effective methodology to draw up check objectives by attaining them with all levels of the person and predisposing for their success through the analysis and visualization of achievement.

TYPES OF PEOPLE ACCORDING TO NEUROLINGUISTIC PROGRAMMING

Visuals: they need to see and be looked at. The vision is the last developed sense and the characteristic of the human species is mostly oriented to it, it is a kind of constant in the species of the last developed sense, which is the one that is most used or that all revolves around it. These types of people are fast and can even skip words because of the speed of their thinking, as thought wins over the word. They generally have the highest voice volume , their thinking is mostly with images.

Auditory : with an intermediate rhythm, they pause when they speak, they need to know that the other is understanding or is listening to them. They think one thing at a time or the thought goes parallel to what they hear or speak. They are usually deeper than the visual ones, but covering fewer things. They are usually conversationalists and do not always look at the interlocutor, but give preference to the auditory field.

Kinesthetic: they need more physical contact. They are more sensitive than the preceding two, their world is precisely that, the sensations, the five senses more as a sensation than as a field of action , mainly at the skin level . The emotional aspect and emotions are very important to them.

HOW CAN NLP BRING YOU TO SUCCESS

Neuro-linguistic programming (NLP) uses both verbal and non-verbal patterns found in language. "Neuro" refers to the mind, "linguistic" language, and "programming" how our behavior and our body are programmed by the mind and the way we phrase things.

The person has a dominant sense: visual, auditory, kinesthetic (touch), olfactory (smell) or gustatory (taste). Generally the NLP relies on the first three.

The concept was coined in the 1970s by Richard Bandler and John Grinder, neuro-linguistic programming. Helping people have wealthier, happier, fulfilling lives was their mission. I used the NLP methods to work with people with phobias, autism, behavioral disabilities, etc. Over the years, neuro-linguistic therapy has become a very effective self-help method in general. Hypnotherapists, public speakers, government officials, and anyone is taking the time to learn the skills are using it today.

So why should you take advantage of the NLP's power?

Neuro-Linguistic Programming (NLP) explores how people think and experience the world. Obviously, with accurate science, something so subjective can not be measured, so it leads to models of how these things work. From these models, strategies have been built to alter the emotions, attitudes and values quickly and effectively that bind you.

That's the NLP's strength. It's a series of methods that allow you to reprogram your mind, helping you to eliminate bad habits or attitudes and replace them with good ones, either in yourself or others.

Keys to the NLP 1. Examine your system of beliefs.

Are you a survivor or a source of success? NLP's designers researched more successful people than others. We reflected on their beliefs and behaviors and discovered that some people believe we can do anything, even if they face some serious hurdles.

Others, on the other hand, assume that they will be victims of bad luck and limited success. "When you know that you are building your inner world, you understand that you can alter it." Which one are you?

2. Choose an anchor.

An anchor is a state of thought, a new cycle of stimulus-response. Identify the way you want to act, like being effective and optimistic, very clearly.

Remember a time when you felt like that and go back to that condition emotionally. I will catch myself in that position if I close my eyes, listen to some quiet music and take a few deep breaths. Be mindful of your listening, tasting, seeing and feeling. Note that you relive experience and circumstance when the condition is best. Check the location sometimes.

I remember a moment when I was twelve years old and making four tackles in a row playing soccer and feeling totally invincible. I can scent the flowers, hear the applause, and feel my pulse in my throat!

3. Put the anchor in place. Visit your anchor again and establish a hand gesture this time to align with your desired state. With their other palm, some people pound their side, strike their throat, or pump their hand into the air.

Practice any people who feel confident for you. Next you will find a word, expression or sound explaining this state of being. Repeat this process several times to create a strong anchor that can be used at any time and start with any of the tools: the hand gesture, the expression, the visualization. Use and use all of them

CHAPTER 2

ETHICS OF COMMUNICATION

Ethical cooperation is important for responsible decision-making and learning. The goal is to create and cultivate partnerships and build communities in and through environments, societies, platforms and media. Ethical correspondence often entails responsibility for the messages you send to others and for the short-term or long-term consequences of your contact.

Whether you're talking to a close friend or talking to the employees at an all-staff meeting, your tone must be real and compatible with your philosophy of importance. The antithesis of honest discourse is cheating the audience and sending a message that is hidden or not real.

In fact, ethical contact may apply to the platform or even the language you choose to convey your message. Using a platform that limits the audience or communicates a message in a language not fully understood by your audience restricts how the message is heard and interpreted. For example, if you talk to a group of staff who are predominantly deaf or hearing impaired, ethical contact includes a sign-language interpreter.

Not only does a communication ethic concern the individual, but businesses, corporations and professional entities are also very concerned about it. For ethical communication practices, a company for unethical communication methods is not as successful as one.

For example, a company with unethical communications practices can withhold evidence that it damages the environment or violates a law through lack of transparency; while a business with ethical communications practices may automatically release a communiqué to the parties concerned.

In this case, disclosure makes the business more successful by notifying its clients, prospective or present, providers / suppliers, or other associates of potential environmental threat or violation of the law.

In other words, in this case, openness will promote loyalty and good faith, so that the successful company will not mask what is in the audience's interest.

For the sake of counterexamples, there may be a period where secrecy is the most effective business practice: consider the trade secrets case, when a design strategy or marketing technique is not disclosed publicly in the interest of competitive advantage; or when terms of agreement / use that a company may have with a service provider preclude disclosure.

THE PRINCIPLE OF ETHICAL COMMUNICATION

There are a number of core principles associated with ethical communication, along with the core value of integrity along with all other beliefs. It can be said, however, that there is a virtue behind integrity (in terms of professional communication) and that is emotional intelligence / empathy as the counterpart of all soft skills, which allows all workers to be heard and communicate effectively with others.

Within the framework of ethical communication, emotional intelligence allows one to understand the needs of others and to meet those needs as efficiently as possible as if in their shoes.

1. To be truthful and honest is to explain to an audience what is believed to be true (only 100% of the facts), with no intention of deceiving or revealing just parts of the evidence. It also means being as objective as possible, i.e. not tailoring the story based on what the author wants to believe the audience.

Letting the listener consider the evidence that is presented honestly and conclude that what they choose to think is a central principle of ethical discourse. Ethical correspondence should be focused on detailed information and facts-do not cheats in a word.

2. Hearing and listening to someone are two different things.

To be effective in ethical communication, the recipient must proactively listen to the speaker and not just hear what they want to hear, or hear only parts of the conversation. This also means asking questions for an explanation if any argument is not fully understood.

3. Speak Non-Judgmentally

Ethically and concisely talking means speaking with each audience in a non-judgmental way, negating unnecessary conflict, which typically results in a communication breakdown and leads to misunderstandings. Unnecessary conflict is never good for any business, and such conflicts usually result from unethical communications, with often the catalyst for such communication breakdowns being judgmental, accusatory, and overly critical comments.

5. Speak From Your Own Experience

It is important to bring your personal experience into a dialog with business listeners, providing something more tangible to back up your arguments. Such a method of communication (experiential communication) paints a complete picture for your audience and helps to prove your points so that the audience understands what is being said better.

5. Consider the recipient's preferred communication channel

If you use a communication channel that your intended recipient does not prefer, you risk losing an audience. Use the most preferred communication channel, be it face-to-face, email, conference call, phone call, messenger app, etc., to communicate effectively with your listeners.

Always, be mindful of the chosen delivery form for that company when delivering data to a business audience, whether it is maps, charts, PowerPoint presentations, etc. Therefore, because body language is very significant, face-to-face meetings with business clients are often desired.

6. Try to Understand

While being diligent in listening is vital, it is also crucial that listeners try to understand fully what is being said before answering. While it is fine to ask for clarity or proof of a claim, questions posed by listeners have been answered many times before. Before constructing an answer, listeners should think about what has been said. Reading "between the lines" is also an important skill that makes it possible to understand what is not being said, but has been implicitly said or implied.

7. Avoid a Negative Voice

Ethically speaking means that the speaker avoids rudeness, is polite and professional, and is tactful, the ethical communicator understands that what you're doing is not just important, but how you're saying it. The tone is one of the communication's most important aspects. If the sound is incorrect, a listener can completely miss the context, which can lead to unnecessary confrontations that reduce the profitability of the company.

Controlling one's language goes hand in hand with self-control, a soft ability that helps one to decide how they want to respond (for example) to a close business message as opposed to the most appropriate way to respond.

Essentially, maintaining the mood optimistic or supportive is better because the listener often takes up the tone of a written message— or one's speech— and can affect how the message is heard and/or interpreted.

In fact, while being honest and open is necessary, patience-and professional wisdom-means understanding when speaking up is unacceptable and when it is vital. Tact also means knowing that being totally honest does not mean being harsh or pessimistic-it is important to be totally honest and open with one's thoughts and feelings while being polite and respectful.

8. Do not disrupt others

It is important to allow others to talk in order to create a peaceful, efficient working environment. Interrupting others leads to misunderstandings and needless disputes and an organizational communication breakdown that only hinders business development and creates problems. Interrupting others not only shows a lack of respect, but does not encourage the listener to fully understand what is being said, which often leads to erroneous theories.

9. Respect for privacy and confidentiality

Most companies should include a clause in their code of ethics that specifies what is acceptable to protect confidentiality and privacy for customers and workers. This can have a wide range of effects, from eliminating rumors in the office and reducing negative discussions about customers and/or staff's private lives.

10. Accept Responsibility

A central tenant is responsible for the actions arising from one's words, whether good or bad, within any acceptable communication context. It encompasses both short-term and long-term interaction implications. Owning one's vocabulary emphasizes the value of an appropriate discourse skill.

EXAMPLES OF ETHICAL COMMUNICATION

There are a number of examples of how ethical communication can affect the result of an issue in a company or organizational environment, showing that ethical communication standards should be followed: medical industry: there is not only the main HIPAA legislation in the medical industry, but there are many medical ethical guidelines that medical professionals have to obey.

Those values guarantee that their rights are protected by all patients and fellow medical professionals. Of example, physicians are required by law not to reveal confidential patient information to anyone who has not consented to private access to such private information.

Property consulting industry: Ethical communications in the property consulting industry can take several forms, including disclosing key pieces of information to prospective homeowners of a property, including "negative" truths about the property— for example, disclosing the entire property history, including any accidents or crimes that occurred on the property.

Marketing industry: Ethical marketing campaigns can include announcing to consumers that their business marketing strategies are not effective and that a cheaper provider or other methods of marketing would yield better results.

Virtually every company can profit from the standards of responsible discourse, which always aims to ensure that every member of the organization can provide useful pieces of information in order to make the best decisions.

HOW TO HOLD A DESCENT CONVERSATION

It is probably one of the most difficult parts of communication to start a conversation with someone. You can find you can easily speak to some men, while talking to others is like pulling teeth. But don't panic—there are a few basic tricks to help you start a good conversation with almost anyone, as well as a few suggestions to launch discussions with specific individuals.

Only follow these steps if you want to learn how to start a good discussion.

MAKE THE PERSON FEEL THAT YOU MATTER.

Just by making him feel like you care about what he has to say and that his opinion matters to you, you will turn a complete stranger into a friend. If the person thinks you're chatting just to hear your own voice, he will instantly be switched off. Instead, turn your body and focus on that person, without being too intense, and keep your eye contact. Give the person some personal space, but prove that the person has your attention.

Make the person feel important about his thoughts. When he starts talking about a subject, ask more questions about it rather than asking about something you really want to talk about.

Use the name of the person once or twice after hearing it.

If the person first speaks, nod attentively to indicate you are listening.

ASK QUESTIONS WITHOUT CHALLENGING THE PERSON

A lot of a good conversation begins with questions, but the person you're talking to shouldn't sound like being interrogated at a police station. Before offering your opinion and actually talking to him or her, do not shoot questions at the guy. Nothing is worse than getting the third degree you get.

Asking too many questions will only make the other person feel awkward and force him to find a way out of the conversation. When you think you've posed too many questions, make a joke. Say, "Sorry, the conversation is over," and think about something else.

Ask the person, not his dreams and desires, about his hobbies or interests.

Anything interesting to talk to, Don't ask the person what he thinks of the latest news disaster or how much he has lately had to work overtime. Enjoy the talk topic as well as the conversation itself.

Just make sure you're distributing. Ideally, you will pay the same number as the other guy.

BE FUNNY.

This doesn't mean you're going to have to do a stand-up routine, just put in some jokes and tell them a funny story to break the ice. You're going to be surprised how funny sharing stories will open up to others. Everybody loves smiling and making others feel relaxed.

This is a fun way to make some stressed people happier and chat with them. Use your humor to get the attention of the guy. Display that you're fast on your feet with wordplay, funny jokes, and general banter.

If you've got a funny story about a murderer, use it as long as it's brief. You haven't told a long story before or you may fall flat on your face.

ASK OPEN ENDED QUESTIONS.

Open-ended questions are questions that require a response of more than a yes or no. Open-ended questions enable people to comment, enabling dialogue. You draw out the person and make him part of a conversation. As opposed to questions with yes or no answers, open-ended questions bring growth to a conversation.

MAKE SURE THAT THE QUESTIONS ARE FULLY OPEN.

Don't ask the person what he thinks is life's meaning; just ask what he thinks about this year's Lakers ' season.

Also, you will know when the discussion is not going on. If somebody gives you yes or no answers to questions that need more answers, the person may not be interested in talking to you.

Remember what not to do. There are a couple of ways to kill any good conversation before it can blossom. If you want to learn how to start a good conversation, you can stop a few basic things right from the start.

DON'T SHARE OVERLY PERSONAL DETAILS.

Don't talk about your painful breakup, the strange rash on your back, or how you start wondering if anybody really loves you in your life. To people who really know you well, you can save that.

Don't ask anything that could lead to an awkward answer from the individual. Let the person talk about his other, profession or wellbeing, which is important. Don't wonder if someone meets just to figure out that he's got his heart broken lately.

DON'T THINK ABOUT YOURSELF ALL THE TIME.

If you're droning on and on how nice you're or what you're going to have for breakfast the next day, the person can quickly lose interest, though poking fun at yourself and giving some personal information can put the other person at ease.

PAY ATTENTION.

Do not forget the name, employment, or any important information discovered by the individual after five minutes. This will make you feel like you don't care about anything at all. Say it loudly when the person says his name, so you are more likely to remember it.

TIPS FOR A BETTER CONVERSATION
FOCUS ON THE CONVERSATION

If you are talking to someone, focus on that. If you have a thousand things in your head, the conversation doesn't interest you too much for whatever reason, don't have it. It's that clear. If we want to have a conversation that really brings us, that is productive for both parties, we must leave everything to pay maximum attention. So nothing about mobile phones, television, mental notes about pending tasks, etc. etc.

DON'T GO EXPERT

Between providing a piece of information and going expert, there is an important difference. Do you understand the nuance, right? To have a good conversation you have to assume that you always have something to learn from the other .

If you think that you are the greatest expert in something, it will not take long to realize that you are not the one who knows most about your specialty, and that there are people who know a lot about many other things. On this subject I really liked Seth Godin's post: "

Everyone is better than you , ..." in something. And the same happens to the rest.

That is, you will be better than the other person in something, and vice versa. Let's take advantage of this reality, to get something positive out of each conversation. The key is to go with an open mind, think that you can always learn something from each conversation, until you end up giving your opinion, so that the other party expresses itself more freely. You will have time to respond and argue.

USE OPEN AND GENERIC QUESTIONS

The more open the question, the more you will make him think and the more interesting his answer will be. If you are specific you end up guiding the answer. It is not the same to ask, were you afraid yesterday? How did you feel? With the first question, the answer will stick to fear, and set aside other feelings you might experience.

LET THE CONVERSATION FLOW

For a conversation to take on a life of its own, it is important that it flows, that it is a continuous 'give and take' in which ideas go alone. If you insist on recovering that data, that anecdote that you had in mind, you stop listening and also when you release it, you will hinder the conversation . If it made sense 1 minute ago, it is most likely that I don't have it that much now. Let go of that 'phrase'. The opportunity will come again, or not. Never mind.

IF YOU DON'T KNOW SOMETHING, ACKNOWLEDGE IT

You have no obligation to know everything. You don't have to be the expert

DON'T COMPARE YOUR EXPERIENCES WITH YOURS

Sometimes it may seem empathy, but we are really trying to divert the conversation. We are trying to regain control. If they are telling us something, it is for us to listen to them. Not for us to compare his suffering / success with ours. We will never live things the same way as the other person.

DON'T REPEAT YOURSELF

When we have a clear argument, we tend to repeat it n times. In the same way or with different approaches, but with the sole objective of making our point of view clear again and again

That you say it once is enough. If you doubt if the other person has understood it, it is better to ask him, have you understood my point of view? how about,...?

SKIP THE DETAILS

The other party has not come to learn statistics, historical data or on the contrary unimportant details that contribute nothing to the conversation. He has come to see you. Besides, people don't care too much about the details.

LISTENS

We prefer to talk to listen. It allows us to have the situation under control and not get confused.

"Most of us do not listen with the intention of understanding, but with the answer"

To get positive things out of a conversation, we have to be present, pay attention, forget the rest, if you're not willing to do it, why do you have that conversation?

BE BRIEF

Bring value with what you say, listen eagerly to understand and learn and be concise. "A good

conversation is like a miniskirt. Short enough to
maintain interest, and long enough to cover the matter.
"

CHAPTER 3

BEHAVIORAL PSYCHOLOGY

Behavioral psychology is the study of the relationship between our mind and our behavior. Sometimes we hear behavioral psychology called behaviorism. Researchers and scientists studying behavioral psychology are trying to understand why we act in our way.

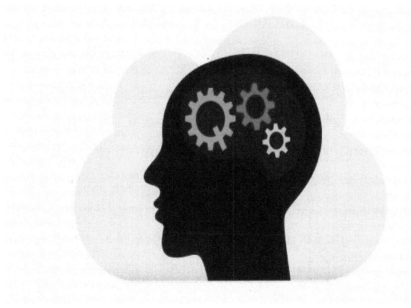

They are interested in discovering our behaviors and patterns of behavior. If we can use behavioral psychology to predict human behavior, we hope that we can build better habits as individuals, create better products as companies, and develop better living spaces as communities

PROMINENT BEHAVIORISTS

The field of behavioral psychology was developed by several prominent behaviorists. A publication called "Psychology as the Behaviorist See It," written by John B. Watson in 1913, was the first description of behaviorism and brought the theory to light. Other well-known behaviorists included B. F. Skinner, who has developed the operant conditioning hypothesis.

The proofs of behavioral psychology are stated as one's environment affects their actions directly. Through observing and monitoring the environment of a person, actions can be assessed and adjusted effectively. As John B. Watson claimed in his 1913 article, behaviorists claim you might turn them into adults with the habits of your choosing if you take 20 children and raise them in a specific environment.

Conditioning

The most engaging thing from behavioral psychology study is conditioning theory, definition, and implementation. There are two types of conditioning: working conditioning and standard conditioning. You will quickly recognize the parallels between these ideas by researching these two different types of learning and how teachers and parents teach children.

Classical Conditioning

An occurring organic stimulus is added together with a neutral stimulus to generate a reaction in classical conditioning. Finally, while the external stimulus is no longer present, the neutral stimuli must generate the reaction. For starters, if your alarm goes off on a school day, let's presume you want to teach a child to get ready right away and come down to the kitchen. The warning is the stimulus that occurs naturally, and the neutral stimulus would be getting dressed. Eventually, after rising, the child would be so used to getting dressed that they will continue even in the case of the alarm blowing. This is regarded as a conditioned response.

Most often, this form of conditioning is used to build new habits or break bad habits and is largely based on comparisons. Another well-known behaviorist, Ivan Pavlov, demonstrated the effectiveness of classical dog conditioning. If confronted with food, dogs are salivating. Pavlov put a bell in the milk, then a lab coat. Finally, the dogs were only salivated by the sight of the lab coat.

Modern learning is not dumb. There is a phenomenon called extinction that breaks from the relationship that produced the conditioned response. How soon this can happen depends on a number of factors, such as the frequency of the stimuli in the first steps of conditioning, and how long the conditioning lasts.

The most widely used form of behavioral psychology is operant conditioning. It is used by parents, teachers, and employers themselves. The behavior is either rewarded or punished by operant conditioning. Sound familiar? Each action has a consequence. The target will avoid the action if that result is consistently bad. If the outcome is successful, the action will be replicated. This is the basis for our society's way of teaching girls. It is also often used in animal training.

Operating conditioning is also primarily based on experiences. In this case, associations are built on the basis of behavioral consequences. The behavior will either be intensified or removed if a certain behavior is correlated with a single outcome.

The most vital thing about operant conditioning is: each time the relationship is to be formed, the result must be the same. This is why it is often said that parents are persistent in their penalties and incentives. It is critical that the result of operant conditioning is the same or highly similar any time the target behavior is introduced.

Partial reinforcement may be applied after a behavior is learned. For example, when you build the habit, you might reward your child every time they do the dishes, but after the habit is built, you might only reward the child with an allowance or some kind of treat every week. Partial reinforcement is important during the initial stages of operant conditioning, as the connections require continuous strengthening.

Common Applications

Although the behavioral study has declined sharply since the 1950s, there are still certain applications in use today. Some of these apps, particularly for parents or pet owners, will seem very familiar.

Behavioral psychology is used in many situations in therapeutic applications. The most common way to use behaviorism is to treat children with autism or disturbance. Combined with conditioning, behavioral analysis can help children with autism and other mental disabilities to learn new skills and techniques. Aversion therapy, contingency management, and systematic desensitization are other ways in which behavioral psychology is applied to therapeutic practices.

Adults making and Changing Habits will also benefit from certain aspects of behavioral psychology. It is behavioral psychology that forms the way in which people break bad habits or create new healthy habits.

Every book, article, tip, and trick you're reading about habit making or breaking is based on behavioral psychology. Habits are usually created by traditional conditioning, whereas bad habits are disrupted by conditioning the operant.

Teaching children Behavioral psychology in today's society has shaped how we teach our children. The whole structure of public schools is focused on conduct. Children are praised for learning, and relationships are formed to help them learn new skills, knowledge, and behaviour. Families use operational conditioning to teach their kids right from wrong and to teach them household and community rules. The way we raise our children might look very different without the developmental psychology studies that took place between 1910 and 1950.

Strengths And Weaknesses When it comes to behavioral psychology, there are some strengths and weaknesses to remember. Behaviorism's shortcomings are the reason why it is no longer seriously studied. Psychologists over the past few years have concentrated more on evolutionary neuroscience and how our brain and desires play a role in our behavior.

Attributes One of behaviorism's main strengths is that behavior is an objective, tangible activity. Behavior can be seen and evaluated in relation to feelings, perceptions, and moods. It makes it easier than with other forms of psychology to identify and gather data. Such abilities have continued to use behaviorism to build a variety of therapies that benefit children and adults alike.

Weaknesses Now, most researchers say the behavior is a one-sided way of looking at actions. An individual mood, thoughts, and feelings that play a role in human behavior do not matter. Many researchers also argue that free will is not taken into consideration by behaviorism.

There are also other forms of instruction that do not require reinforcement or punishment, and these approaches are not taken into account by behaviorism. Individuals can also change their actions based on new information, even if this information has not been introduced by conditioning or is contradictory to a previously conditioned response.

UNDERSTAND BEHAVIORAL PSYCHOLOGY TO WIN IN BUSINESS AND RELATIONSHIPS

How to Know Behavioral Psychology Can Improve Your Company Blossom Behavioral Psychology (or Behavioral

Psychology) is a "scientific approach that applies the study of psychology to measured or observed behavior."

In understanding human behavior, you increase your chances of success in your company. Whomever your passion, whomever path you seek— building a business, getting married, raising a family, traveling the world— whatever you think your nirvana is, there are six simple, fundamental needs that make us work and motivate all human behavior.

What are the six human needs that we all share?

• Certainty / comfort: confidence that discomfort and happiness can be avoided

• Uncertainty / variety: the need for unexpected, change and new stimulation

• Significance: feeling distinctive, significant, exceptional or necessary

• Love / Connection: a strong sense of closeness or union with someone or something

• Growth: capacity growth, capability or awareness

• Contribution: a sense of duty and an emphasis on helmets. Personalization makes people happy

A curious personalization test was tracked concerning waiters and mints with three control groups:

• The first group saw waiters passing out mints alongside the check while not discussing the mints. It improved tips against the control group by around 3 points.

• The second group saw waiters distributing two mints by hand (separate from the check) and pointing them directly to the tables. This saw a 14 percent increase in tips.

• The last party had a few minutes of waiters carrying out the check. Shortly later, waiters came back with another package of mints and let customers know that just in case they had taken out more mints. This category saw a 23 percent increase in tips.

3. Do it to others...

In your entire life, you have certainly been reminded of the Golden Rule: "Do to others as you would have them do to you." While this is sound advice, does it extend to your business?

Absolutely

If you're doing something for someone else, they're usually going to return the favor. The principle of reciprocity can be used in industry, for example by giving away personalized coffee mugs or free trials for 30 days. Even saying' thank you' can be a small but important way to build a loyal advocate community.

4. Provide a novel experience The need for the unknown is always remembered by people. Yes, this argument has long been supported by scientists. "The midbrain region controls our motivation levels and our ability to predict incentives by producing dopamine in the brain's frontal and temporal regions is a well-known fact by scientists.

We have now shown that novelty activates this brain area. "This explains why people are waiting in line for a new iPhone and paying hundreds of dollars even if they already have a perfectly functional model. They want a novel experience and the newest features.

5. "In 1975, researchers Worchel, Lee and Adewole wanted to know whether people would value cookies in two identical glass jars," "One jar housed ten cookies, while the other one had only two stragglers." Obviously, participants were drawn to the near-empty jar because of the basic psychological theory of supply and demand.

HOW TO CODIFY THOUGHTS

Ideas do not become the leadership of thinking until they are codified and written down.

You may have brilliant ideas or know how to help people in very tangible ways, but if it's stuck in your brain, your knowledge is lost.

What members say otherwise is to codify their skills.

A thought leader is a voice that can monetize their knowledge in a specific topic. "Monetize your skills" is the key phrase in that description. If you want to get paid for your experience, you need to codify it. It involves tracking your thoughts regularly so that they can spread past you.

Secure Your Expertise What would it be if you shared your best advice?

Everyone has five to seven things they know are real. These are the central principles of your experience, and when solving problems or giving advice you naturally gravitate.

For eg, 3% Rule The 3% Rule is one of my core ideas. The law claims that 3 percent of your audience is buying at any given time, the majority is not. I make extensive use of the Law in my life. In my book, Sticky Branding, it's a philosophy and a tool I use in my consulting and speech.

The 3 percent rule is a simple idea, but codifying the pattern took me a while. Several iterations have passed to make it a shareable tool that can be used by anyone.

You too have the core ideas on which to base your expertise. Take the time to document your core ideas. These are the building blocks of your leadership of thinking.

Making your ideas tangible is also a branding act. The first step to codify your thought leadership is to identify and record your thoughts. The next step is to put together the ideas in order to share them quickly.

Treat as goods the core ideas. Give them a mark or tag and provide a brief statement describing it to each of them. For example, the "3 percent rule" is the name, and the statement is "At any given time you buy 3 percent of your market, the rest is not." Packaging your core ideas has two advantages: Making ideas concrete: Documenting your ideas makes them concrete. This makes the idea a concrete term that you can communicate with others by giving the idea a name and description.

Give gravitas ideas: a clear explanation gives credibility to your ideas. The practice in labeling removes the designer from the product, encouraging the concept to stand alone.

Monetize your leadership in thought Documenting your thoughts makes them concrete. This takes skills that you provide in your workplace or when you swap time for money and transforms them into units that can be traded.

There's meaning in each of the core ideas. They can be converted into keynotes, courses, books, materials for training, or a host of other services. The challenge is to pull them out of your head so you have to work with the building blocks.

STRATEGIES TO DISCOVER WHAT IS IMPORTANT TO YOU

Life, along with myriad challenges and opportunities, offers endless variety. With so many choices, it is easy to get lost in indecision. You want results, but you are uncertain if you're on the right track. You would like your life to be balanced, However, due to many conflicts, we often spend a lot of energy in one direction.

What is happening here is a lack of prioritization, a lack of understanding of what is most important to you in life— and then acting on it. Although not life-threatening, it may erode your quality of life by failing to identify what is most meaningful to you. To ensure having most opportunities to live a full, happy and productive life, your key priorities must be at zero. Here are a few ways of doing just that.

Identify your life's most important people.

They are important to you when you care about someone. Nonetheless, occasionally we take for granted loved ones, family members, friends and colleagues. This is a disservice both to them and to us. You make a conscious effort to identify and respect these meaningful relationships by naming the most important people in your life. Since man is by nature a gregarious creature, it is a practical, effective way to make the most of life to tend towards those closest to you.

Think of what you enjoy doing the most.

It may be planning floral displays for some, trying out new foods, walking with a loved one at sunset. Others may enjoy most sports and recreational activities, or read books, listen to music, engage in lively discussions. Clearly, something you like doing is important to you. It's more than just spending time or relaxing. When you take the time to decide what you like to do the most, you are more likely to take advantage of those opportunities to make room in your life. You will also rely on that information in the process, in addition to defining what is most important to you.

What are your attributes, skills or talents?

Check out your life and highlight your strengths, abilities or talents? You were great at marbles, ping pong, sledding, multiplication tables, spelling bees, for example, when you were a kid? Have you found yourself exceptional in science or English or mathematics? Are you good at carpentry, planning environments, building things, working out how to fix what's wrong? Through artistic expression, can you forget yourself, making something out of nothing? There is a strong likelihood that these abilities, skills and talents are deeply embedded in what is most important to you.

Count the greatest accomplishments and achievements.

In line with evaluating what you think you're doing well, take some time to identify your achievements. Whether it's a huge achievement or something small, it doesn't matter. That counts is the impression you were offered by the outcome. You feel joy and satisfaction in life when you are proud and excited about your accomplishments. It's also a good indication that this is important to you.

Tell the best qualities of your friends, loved ones and family members.

You may think you know the best qualities or talents, but you may overestimate or underestimate what's right for you. In fact, when it comes to self-analysis, you're not very critical. That's why it's enlightening to ask those who know you best what they consider is your best qualities. For example, you might find that you have a keen analytical ability, something that you haven't tapped or put to good use. Perhaps the most impressive thing is your kindness.

Or, the fact that you listen well and in a way that is empowering and uplifting, support others. If you know what these characteristics are, you will decide what to do to take advantage of them, if anything. Something is important to you here. It may be a painless way to figure this out by telling others to help you recognize them.

While it may be hard, because it's too tough, you don't have to lose a target.

The most disturbing thing is someone who gives up as they are about to achieve their goal. We've always done so, not because we like to say that it's anything. Those targets, of course, are incredibly challenging. These are complex, costly, these require an excessive amount of time, or they need hard-to-reach support and allies.

The trick to holding fast to a nearly unreachable target is to break it into bits. Distinguish it and identify steps or stages. Through concentrating on the next step rather than the final goal, it is easier to make the requisite commitment to see through this process. You're going to go through different stages on the way to the goal over time. That's how even the most difficult task is reached

You can still make ends meet and fulfill your goals.

You may be trapped in a position that you don't like. You did it because you needed the money and because things haven't changed financially, because you can't see a way ahead. It's time to break this dead-end mentality and chart a plan for making improvements that will allow you both to follow your goals and take care of your financial responsibilities. You may decide to go back to school for further training or to obtain or complete a degree.

What you are doing in the process, the people you meet, the opportunities to which you are introduced, will make a profound difference in your outlook. Remember; make sure to optimize your sporting and leisure activities. When you like skiing, plan a few ski trips. If painting is your power, get the medium of your choosing busy making.

Work with depression or anxiety in a constructive manner that may have been in the way of doing what you want.

A natural part of life is a transient depression or fear. The emotions that encourage us to make necessary changes, although not without discomfort, Nonetheless, persistent stress or anxiety will be alleviated only with professional assistance. It may be in order to have the treatment and/or therapy. If you find that these powerful emotions stand in the way of doing what is most important in life for you, you owe it to yourself and your loved ones to get the help you need.

Get over the sensation of not being strong enough.

Most of us felt the sting of rejection, either because we didn't live up to our own or someone else's standards. Overt or covert criticism, biting or harsh comments, the gradual removal of friends and colleagues adds to the sinking feeling that we are not good enough. Nevertheless, we are not determined by others, and we should never encourage them to behave as they can.

The only way you can be strong enough is to think you are. Since no one can make you do anything and only decide how to live, choose the positive and uplifting alternative. Choose what gives you the best chance of achieving the desired outcome. Give it your utmost care, attention and determination.

You're not going to be good enough if you do the best you can. In reality, you're going to be better than good enough. Wherever you want to go, you'll be right.

What happens to you? Do that. Do that.

Good luck is like sunshine. It makes you feel good, warmly bundles you up, and it costs nothing. But how many times do you walk away from happiness and engage in some boring, uninvolving, repetitive, endless or unproductive task or activity instead?

Think about what makes you happy if you want to be happy in life. Find a way in your everyday life to incorporate your task or operation. Walking in nature, working in the garden, whipping up a culinary delight, playing with the kids, making your partner love,

Whatever it is, this is important to you, something that you greatly appreciate. Make sure you do it as often as you can, with the full presence of the moment and the joy you can have

STRATEGIES TO IMPROVE (OR ELIMINATE) BAD RELATIONSHIPS

HOW TO AVOID BAD RELATIONSHIPS A stable relationship is marked by loyalty, confidence, integrity, good communication and the willingness of each partner to preserve his or her individuality and identity. The inverse of all these aspects will describe a poor or abusive partnership — disrespect, dishonesty, deceit, lack of communication, and pressure to change who you are for your spouse.

Such not - so-great traits may sometimes involve healthy relationships, but only for very short periods of time. If the relationship in which you are having any of these' symptoms' on a regular basis, you are likely to be in a bad relationship that needs to end for significant periods of time.

In every friendship you have right from the beginning, learn to recognize these negative signs.

Determine what really makes you happy. What does friendship really matter to you? What are the beliefs in a relationship you need to maintain? What are you serious about the need to honor your partner? In reality, what things make you feel good and you would like to stay in a relationship? Try not to focus on the negatives (that is, what makes you crazy or unhappy). Concentrate on the positive. Focus on things that really please you — make you feel comfortable inside, make you happy, and don't put stress on you.

Think these things seriously, and write them down. You may need a good time to think about it all.

Read through your list back. In any friendship, these are the things you want and need. These items are not expected to be negotiable.

Learn from the past. Repeatedly having bad relationships can be quite straightforward because you don't take the time to find out what went wrong in your previous relationships. Stop and think about all your past relationships before you enter a new relationship. How many did you end up being bad and unhealthy? Why have they ended up like this? What was it that wasn't working for you about your partner? What was the work of things?

Talk about your relationship's emotional needs and whether previous relationships fulfill those needs. If they weren't, why? What's been missing? What would you want your friend to see?

Talk only if you've got a partner who really' gets' you. Did your partner understand your quirks and appreciate them? Did the things you've been adamant about help your partner? What would you like your wife to think about you?

Look for patterns of interactions with your history. Have all of your partners had the same traits of personality? Have you been moving the relationship too fast? Those trends are the ones that you need to stop in future relationships because they don't work for you.

Slowly begin new relationships. There's no need to rush into a relationship. If you meet someone you think may be a good partner for the first time, see them often— not often. Treat it gently. If you have a history of bad relationships, you may have too much attachment, too fast.

Get to know the person over time this time around. Don't become (yet) dependent on anything on this new person. Be mindful of your actions. Try not to make impulsive decisions.

Remember that love is not equivalent to physical attraction. Strong and sometimes sudden physical attraction. It has the ability to overpower the senses and lead to bad decisions. The physical attraction is, in some situations, the starting point for a long-term, loving relationship. In other cases, love is mistaken for physical attraction.

You may not be able to distinguish between the attention you need and the attention you want if you're in a state of mind where you want attention. Despair and need are not safe. If you're in a poor or vulnerable situation, don't make your big relationship decisions, as you'll most likely make the decision for wrong reasons.

Keep your autonomy. Wherever you are in a partnership, some of your dignity must be retained. It not only means that you have a healthy relationship while preserving your individuality, but it also lets you build healthier attachments.

If you have had one or more bad relationships in the past, because it's safer, you may be tempted to become dependent on your mate easily. But once you get too close, it can be difficult to pull apart again — and the signs of a bad relationship can be more difficult to notice.

Holding your liberty always means keeping and making time for your new circle of friends. Your mates should not be compromised by friendship. They should be accompanied by a friendship. Take advantage of your circle of friends when you're thinking about starting a new relationship and lean on them for support.

Get an objective view. Sometimes it's tough for the trees to see the wood. We are so close to our own memories that we can not critically interpret them — particularly when it comes to emotions. Get the advice of a close friend or family member when you're talking about starting a new relationship.

Anyone who is capable of being objective and has no self-interest linked to your potential partner or relationship. An impartial third party may be able to see things that you clearly did not notice about your potential relationship.

Not just to make sure you don't get into a bad relationship, this sort of objective opinion. Often, this objective opinion is useful in ensuring that you have a good relationship. You may be reluctant to start a relationship with someone who doesn't have the same traits as your old partners, but that's a good thing in fact.

Build the expectations that are realistic. Another tragic causes people to end up in bad relationships over and over again is due to negative thinking. When you think negatively, it will happen the odds are something bad.

And when it does, it actually confirms what you're saying would happen. In other words, you're setting up for failure (perhaps without even knowing it).

Build a list of positive (and realistic) goals before entering into a relationship. Based on the analysis of yourself (i.e. what you are satisfied with) and on the analysis of your past relationships (i.e. what hadn't worked before).

You're not a survivor, you're not meant to be one. You may be more attentive to being a survivor, but it is the wrong kind of concern. You don't want you to be sorry for people. You want people to be happy with you.

Just because in the past you've had bad luck doesn't mean that you're unlucky. You are not meant to have bad relationships at all times. You may change your life's course, but it may mean you have to take a small leap of faith or a chance.

Learn about the early signs of a poor relationship. Many types of relationships may be dysfunctional, but the co-dependent relationship is a particularly bad type. A co-dependent relationship is one in which one partner allows or supports the under reach, irresponsibility, immaturity, addiction, procrastination, or poor health of the other partner. The burden is basically borne by the so-called' supportive' partner. And this partner rarely learns from their actions by not having the' sponsored' partner to suffer repercussions.

Unfortunately, this kind of relationship will carry on the' supportive' partner a horrific toll and become an emotional and physical burden (not to mention financial).

The' supportive' partner ultimately creates a deep animosity toward the' sponsored' partner because they don't pull their weight. Unfortunately, of course, one party is not responsible for the mistake.

The partner that is' sponsored' is no better off. This companion creates a' supporter' such a strong sense of dependency that it becomes impossible to function independently.

Relationships should be healthy in general. When you begin to notice that your potential partner always seems to be' coming to rescue' or that you always need to be' rescued,' this is not a good sign.

RECOGNIZING AN UNHEALTHY RELATIONSHIP Give respect to one another. The foundation of any partnership should be love. It ensures that there is no need for each partner of the partnership to influence or exploit the other person. No one should feel the need to make the other person feel bad, embarrassed or mocked in a healthy relationship.

And if it's a romantic relationship, sex shouldn't be used as a weapon or instrument, and should only happen when both people want it.

Confide in each other. Confidence comes in multiple formats. The other partner should always feel respected by each partner in a partnership. It includes the trust that no deception takes place; the faith that no one is disrespectful; and the confidence that each partner can have secrets without feeling guilty.

Feel comfortable and secure with each other. All partners must feel safe and secure around each other in each relationship. When in the presence of the other, especially of any form of violence, no one should feel scared or nervous.

This also involves no one expressing any doubt that the other party will have a temper that will unexpectedly erupt and result in hitting or throwing stuff.

Fairly settle disputes. Conflicts in any relationship can exist. Healthy relationships, though, can expend more time away from a dispute than in one. In a healthy relationship, if a conflict occurs, it should be handled with dignity and without any lasting damage. Conflict in an unhealthy relationship may seem to be settled, but you may find that it has not been adequately resolved upon closer examination.

Compromises are sometimes needed, but in favor of one partner, it should not always be weighted.

Supporting one another: With whatever they choose to do (or not to do), each person in the relationship should be able to support the other. This also ensures that each partner should be able to express themselves and their thoughts without thinking about negative effects. It's all right not to like something that your friend does or does, but to help it, you don't have to like something.

For your partner's sake, you should never have to risk your own happiness.

To be able to support your friend also means not to comply with anything. This is particularly true when that' something' will harm or kill the partner. For instance, not deciding to have another drink from your partner because your partner needs to drive home Respect the friends and interests of your partner. Both members have other healthy friendships in a healthy relationship. Before the relationship started, every person in a relationship should be able to continue the friendships they had. And none of the relationship members should criticize friendships or disrespect friends.

No member of a healthy relationship, because of their partner, should feel the need to be isolated from family and friends.

When one partner member thinks that the other person is in a dysfunctional marriage, it should say something. It should be handled in a manner that is respectful, not critical, though.

Respect the privacy of one another. Growing participants in a healthy relationship must realize that some details need to be kept private by each partner. Not for reasons of deceit, but simply because the life of no one is an open book. Protection does not include any partner feeling compelled to communicate with the other party any phone call, email or text they get. And no partner will assume that if something is kept private, the other will become jealous and possessive.

Respecting the privacy of each other is related to trusting one another.

CHAPTER 4

HOW TO ANALYZE PEOPLE

It is the knowledge of the character by the features of the face and hand. It is about moving from an empirical art to an observation science. The character is not independent of the physical constitution. It is conditioned by the state of our body, as on the other hand, the body is influenced by the emotions of the soul.

Life is due to a double movement: a dilation movement and a conservation movement; which allows analyzing the personality of any human being.

The Dilation-expansion: It is characterized by its adaptability to the environment, an externalization of intuitive and affective tendencies, sociability, cheerful humor, need to be in groups, intelligence adapted to the useful and directed to practical realizations.

The Conservation-Seclusion: It manifests itself in the opposite way, with an elective adaptation to a privileged environment. Since withdrawal is a defense process, it acts only in a medium that does not suit you.

While the expansive individual is a friend of the whole world, disperses his activity in all directions, reacts impulsively, is determined and has a sensory intelligence of immediate contact, the withdrawn has only friends of choice and if he does not have them he prefers loneliness , he concentrates and is only active in some directions, it is not resolved unless he has reflected, does not trust his sensory impressions and is more idealistic replacing reality with abstractions, distrusts his senses and his reason.

The Expansive individual: It is characterized by having a thick structure, colored and warm skin, wide round face, large mouth, snub nose, large eyes and smiling expression, with ease and abundance of exchanges.

The retracted individual: It is thin in nature, short limbs, dry and cold skin and pale dye. The face is elongated, narrow and bony, it is parsimonious, selective in the exchanges, small mouth, narrow and bony nose, sunken eyes, hermetic face and little communicative.

The Expansive-Retracted: It is an intermediate of the previous two, the face is rectangular, large eyes slightly sunken. It opens or closes depending on the situation.

PHYSIOLOGICAL TRICKS TO ANALYZING PEOPLE

In valuing people we have just met, we are often victims of our own psychological mechanisms. This can lead to misunderstandings and preconceptions that eventually affect our ability to socialize.

The best way to counteract these mistakes is to know how to identify them, so here are the common mistakes we make when valuing others.

1. Confuse personality and situations

When we observe a certain behavior of someone, we immediately think that they act according to their personality. When we think about our own behavior, instead, we usually value it based on the situation in which we find ourselves.

80

For example, we know that we are distant when we are worried about something. However, if a person you just met acts in this way, you may directly assume that he is a jerk.

To avoid falling into this trap, we should always take into account the so-called situational conditions when valuing other people.

2. Confirmation bias

Once we have a certain idea about someone, we usually see everything they do through the filter of these preconceptions.

For example, if you consider a co-worker to be selfish, you look at the behaviors that confirm it, but not on those who deny it.

Although our first impressions are usually quite reliable, they are not infallible, so it is important to review our judgments as we continue to relate to that person .

The best way to counteract confirmation bias is to seek evidence that challenges your initial assumptions actively. Psychology calls this process "positive DE confirmation of expectations."

3. The wavy effect

The wavy effect is a cognitive bias whereby we make a generalization wrong from a single characteristic of the person.

The variable that most causes this effect is physical attractiveness, that is, we tend to value more positively those people who seem attractive to us. Similarly, we also tend to value better those who resemble us.

An effective way to understand how it works is to identify when it occurs in critical situations. For example, when you hire someone for a job or when you are in a situation that involves many new people. If we pay attention, we will see that, in both cases, our tendency is to gravitate towards those people with whom we share certain features, whether physical or cultural background.

4. Let us influence the past

A bad experience with a postal officer can lead us to assess all civil servants negatively. In the same way, knowing a person who reminds us of someone from our past can influence our judgment about that new person.

For example, if the most undesirable person in your class at the school was named Alberto, you will have more difficulty positively assessing a person with that name.

One way to avoid this negative influence is to pay attention to the proportionality of our reactions and identify when we approach a situation with a negative or defensive attitude.

5. The supposed similarity bias

Usually, we tend to assume that others think like us and have our same preferences.

But obviously this is a mistake.

If you want to skip this type of cognitive prejudice is to create a habit of warning people about diversity in people's preferences and expectations. That is, give people the opportunity to let you know that their comfort zone is different from yours.

SECRETS OF HOW TO ANALYZE A PERSON

You surely wanted to be able to read the minds of other people more than once. With the aid of their formed instincts, some are spared, but if you are not so perceptive, you have only one way out: learn to decode the language of the body.

It's no longer a secret that we get 55% of the information with the aid of nonverbal communication.

Face expressions, motions and actions of the body will strip the disguise from anyone and reveal their true thoughts and feelings.

1. Closing your eyes If a person closes his eyes, talking to you, you must know that he is trying to hide or protect himself from the outside world. That doesn't mean I'm scared of you. Alternatively, the other way around, He wants to take you out of his dream area. You may already have bored it. Open and bam your head! You're done.

2. Protecting the mouth by hand It's a vivid example from childhood that we all come. Remember, when you didn't want to say anything, you covered your mouth with the palm of your hand. It's the same person. Many fingertips, fist or palm allow us to express the words. Sometimes with a feigned cough we mask it.

3. Biting the rim of your glasses: Does your buddy intentionally bit his glasses rings? Try to encourage and support him. He must surely be concerned about something and he wants to feel safe at his subconscious level, as in childhood with the breast of the mother. By the way, the same applies to a pencil, pad, finger, cigarette or even chewing gum in hand.

4. Most women use this gesture to draw men's attention. Supporting the head on the extended paws, we reveal our face to show it, as if it were the shop window in a restaurant, as if we were saying, "I am so pretty here, admire me." This act should be noted by people so as not to miss the opportunity to give a timely comment.

5. Stroking the chin The person is trying to make a decision this way. Your attention can be focused downwards, sideways, to the left or to any other side at the same time. He doesn't know what he sees at that exact moment because he's totally immersed in his feelings.

6. Crossed arms One of the most repeated movements. It is not shocking that with this posture many people feel very comfortable, as this gesture helps separate

themselves from others. When we're not happy with something, we use it several times. The crossed arms are a clear sign of your interlocutor's negative attitude.

7. Self-exposure This posture is more accessible, right? When a woman wants to like a friend, by revealing her best sides, she starts to reveal herself. She straightens and bends her thighs to show her breasts. The folded arms below are a clear signal of the interlocutor's attention.

8. Leaning forward Normally he leans forward when a person feels concern for his or her interlocutor and needs to have contact with him or her. The feet that remain in the same place at the same time, but the body moves unconsciously.

9. Leaning back If the individual leans against his seat's back, he makes it clear that the conversation is boring. In your interlocutor's company, you can feel uncomfortable.

10. That's right. Toe, heel Yes, there are also men. Not just youth. This gesture shows the person is very worried.

11. That's right. Rubbing his hands The hands are said to express the emotions of the brain. Generally we show hopes or hope of some success in something when we rub our palms. In other words, when we speak about future benefits, we make this motion.

12. 12. Handshake "glove" It indicates you can trust him if your interlocutor embraces you with both paws.

13. That's right. Squeeze with palm up The palm up displays sensitivity, protecting the face of the interlocutor, but only if it is achieved at once. If for a certain moment the hands were already holding and then somebody placed the hand palm up, it may signify a desire to show who is in charge.

14. 14. Through raising the caller's back, it's as if you spoke about your willingness to help him.

Fifteen. Squeeze with a touch The person can touch the forearm, elbow or back of the person he greets with the available hand. This personal space invasion shows the need for contact. And the smaller the body becomes, the more important it is.

16. Straightening the bond It depends on the situation here. If it's a man who does it in a woman's presence,

he may very much like it. But this gesture can also mean the person is not feeling comfortable. You may have been lying or just wanting to leave.

17. Collecting non-existent hair The gesture of repression is thus called. We use it most of the time to express their overt dissatisfaction. We don't express their opinion freely, in other words, but we certainly don't agree with what's going on around them.

18. Feet on the table This expression can mean a lot of things: bad manners, arrogance, the desire to show off as a great boss or a health concern. Nonetheless, psychologists tend to believe that it would be safer if you use it at home or in the company of your relatives, even if you are very confident in this role.

19. 19. Riding the chair A chair is not a saddle, and the back is not a shield, although it seems to be in some respects. It was also designed for other uses. This way of sitting around is troubling so many people, so we feel a lot of hostility from the "hung" individual at the intuitive level. This position is usually used by powerful men.

20. One of the most attractive female poses is to play with the shoe Cross-legged. And if we apply to him playing the half-removed foot, we make it even more accentuated. This gesture speaks of a happy, peaceful atmosphere and acts as a sort of green human traffic light. 21. Eye contact The eyes are the soul's mirror as well as a natural interactive device. There we can read all the interlocutor's feelings and emotions. Lovers look at each other's heads, expecting unintentionally to see how they get larger. And this shows a lot as, relative to their normal state, the pupils will increase in size up to four times. And, by the way, if the person gets mad, because of the full reduction of the pupils, their eyes become like accounts.

CHAPTER 5
BODY LANGUAGE

Body language is a method of nonverbal communication in which the meaning is conveyed or communicated through bodily actions as opposed to words. This behavior includes expression of the face, the stance of the body, gestures, movement of the hand, touch and space use. In both animals and humans, body language exists, but this article focuses on interpretations of the language of the human body. It's also called kinesics.

Body language should not be confused with sign language, because sign languages are complete languages such as spoken languages and have their own complicated grammar structures, as well as being able to display the fundamental properties that occur in all languages. Body language, on the other hand, does not have a grammar structure and must be understood loosely, rather than having an absolute meaning relating to it.

There are agreed-upon interpretations of a specific behavior in a society. Interpretations can differ from country to country, or from culture to culture. On this topic, there is debate about the universality of body language. Body language, a nonverbal communication branch, complements social interaction with verbal communication.

In addition, some researchers conclude that nonverbal contact accounts for most of the information exchanged during interpersonal interactions. This helps to define the connection between two individuals and governs behavior, but can be unclear.

THE BENEFITS OF BEING ABLE TO READ OTHER PEOPLE'S BODY LANGUAGE

Body language is the positions, gestures and movements of the whole body that we use to share how we feel or what we do. Given what you can see on tv or read on the Internet, there is no way to use body language to grasp exactly what someone else is doing. Just think about how difficult it can be to play and how fun gesture-based games like Charades. Such games wouldn't be very difficult if decoding body language were that simple and easy.

Our physical activity can reveal a great deal about what we're doing. For instance, if you could only see the arms of a person as they were driving a moving vehicle, you would almost certainly understand that they were driving.

Thanks to their architecture and control systems, the movement associated with driving cars and trucks is very uniform. You would also realize that if you could only see their body movement in profile, someone was floating under water. The gestures associated with the different styles of swimming are unique.

But what if you saw a guy fluttering like a bird in his arms? Would you be able to interpret from that gesture alone what he was doing? Perhaps not. He might play a game, show how birds fly to someone else, attempt to dry himself off, or in an altered state of mind where he thinks he's a bird. These are just a few of the possible interpretations of such action, and this explains why you can not rely solely on body language to interact or appreciate what they are doing with other people.

Body language differs from sign language that can be used to communicate directly and meaningfully in that body language is a natural set of movements whereas sign language is an artificial set of movements given a very specific set of meanings.

Whereas for other people, body language can be vague but interpretable, sign language can only be interpreted by people who have studied its gestures and meanings. The world today uses nearly 7,000 different sign languages, but body language remains practically ubiquitous, even among animal species.

How do we benefit from reading body language?

Watching and reading body language has many valid and normal advantages.

The most important advantages are social: we perceive body language in order to recognize who may be a danger, who may need support, and who behaves in a productive and useful manner. A police officer, for example, might note that someone is "behaving suspiciously" in a typical way with a person who has just committed a crime or who has been stopped by the officer when committing a crime.

Likewise, we will instinctively become suspicious of people who seem to be trailing or closely watching us for no apparent reason, or of people who loiter around a specific location we may be involved in. These are normal reactions to circumstances that are potentially dangerous, although nothing bad happens in most instances.

If you see someone shaking their hands on the ground, you would usually assume that they need assistance. Persons who walk around on their face with a perplexed look may be lost and confused, such as not knowing where they left their car in a large parking lot. An elderly person may attract attention from good

Samaritans in this situation. Hurt or lost and frightened children can sit down and cry.

When you're at work when your supervisor's passing through your room on a job, he or she may avoid watching how you're doing if you seem like you're struggling with a mission; or the manager might break up the kitchen's social circle; or if everyone seems distracted, the boss may sail past you without interrupting anybody.

They also learn to use other methods of using body language. People are more likely to express their feelings of joy or disappointment or their anticipation in comfortable social situations. At sporting events, supporters often yell, run, and pound their fists. Through smiles and enthusiastic movements, people who play fun competitive games like bowling, darts, billiards, etc. will enjoy their victories. They can dominate strut and playfully behave, signaling that they are superior in some way to others around them.

Equally important are our unintended signs. Someone who's upset may be "radiating" messages indicating staying away from me or stopping what you're doing and paying attention to me. In social situations, we focus on body language to express how we feel, not to participate in a complex conversation.

The language of the body always allows us to use electricity. People who fidget or wander back and forth may show an unmet desire, but they "burn off steam" as well. The body feels a need for action, but we are unable to take the necessary action for some reason, and our bodies are going through the motions to fight against invisible constraints.

THE BODY LANGUAGE YOU MUST ABSOLUTELY AVOID

The body language has much more knowledge about how we sound than it can be orally communicated. All the repetitive movements we are making are being perceived subconsciously by others. Depending on the type of body language we use, this can work for or against us. Many movements are transmitting a very positive message, while others are clearly setting a negative tone.

Many people are totally ignorant of their own body language, so they can be quite intimidating in the process of managing such movements. Most of them are reflexive in nature, matching at any given moment automatically with what our minds are thinking.

Nevertheless, we will teach ourselves to solve most of our negative body language patterns with the right information and a little practice.

Practice stopping these negative gestures

- Holding Things in front of your body–a coffee cup, pencil, handbag, etc. Keeping things in front of your body shows shyness and defiance, so you're hidden behind the items in an attempt to distinguish yourself from others. Instead of carrying objects on your side whenever possible, carry them on your side.
- Check the time or check your fingernails–a potent indicator of boredom. Only look at the time you talk to someone. Likewise, avoid the inspection of your fingernails completely.
- Choosing Lint off Your Clothes–If you pick lint off your clothes during a conversation, especially when looking down, most people will assume that you disagree with their ideas and/or are uncomfortable with giving them an honest opinion. Take the lint on its own!

- Stroking Your Chin Looking at somebody– "I judge you! "During the decision-making process, people sometimes rub their cheek. When you smile at somebody while stroking your chin, they will assume you make a judgmental judgement about them.

- Narrowing your eyes–If you want to give somebody the feeling that you don't like them (or their ideas) when staring at them, close your eyes. It places a scowling expression on your face right away. The instinctual, common sign of rage among different species in the animal kingdom (think about the angry faces of lions, wolves, etc.) is a subtle widening of the eyes. Some people make the error of narrowing their eyes as a reflection of thinking during a conversation. Don't send the wrong message to people... don't close your eyes.

- Similar to standing –this only makes people feel awkward. Many people see the 4 square feet of space that cover their body as a personal space. Only with good friends and intimate mates cross this invisible boundary.

- Looking down While in Others ' presence–usually indicates a lack of interest. It is even perceived sometimes as a casual indication of pride. Look straight ahead and get in touch with your mind when you see someone you know.
- Touching your face in a conversation–Face touching is widely perceived as a sign of deceit, particularly on the nose. Often, a traditional move is to cover up the mouth while people are lying. When you talk, keep your hands away from your face.
- Faking a Smile–another frequently used indication of deceit in the face of a scam. A genuine smile twists the eyes ' edges and transforms the whole face's expression. Only the mouth and eyes are used in fake smiles. Differentiating between the two is simple. Unless it's for the video, don't push yourself to smile.
- Leaning Away From Someone You Love–a symbol of isolation and selflessness. Many people may also understand it as meaning: "I don't like you." People tend to lean to people they love and to people they dislike. This is particularly true while sitting around a table. You're giving them the

wrong message if you turn away from someone you like.

- Resting Arms Behind the Head or on the Hips – generally seen as a display of dominance or bigheadedness. Use these movements only when you are in close friends ' presence.
- Not Facing the Person You're Talking To Directly– It suggests a level of discomfort or lack of interest. When we're happily engaged in a chat, we face the person we're referring to squarely between our feet and torso. We prefer to tilt our foot and bodies to the left when we are unaware of the other person or not fully committed to the discussion. During a talk, look straight forward to give the impression that you are genuinely interested in what the other person says.
- Crossing Your Arms–a gesture of defiance to the protection. It may also be viewed by some as a symbol of egotism. Try to keep your arms open and on your hands at all times.
- Displaying a Sluggish Stance–Your stance becomes an instant telltale sign of confidence and calm when you're in an atmosphere full of people. Your place practically makes you stand up,

sending out a clear message of how you should be handled. In the way people react to you, it can make a huge difference. Place your feet apart from each other comfortably, hold back your shoulders, head up and greet people with direct eye contact and a firm handshake.

- Scratching on Your Head and Neck's Backside–a common indication of doubt and uncertainty, It can also be interpreted as a sign of deception. If you communicate with others, try to keep your hands away from your mouth.

- Messing With Your Shirt's Collar–It screams: "I feel awfully anxious and/or awkward! "You keep track of your hands again. Don't stick to it.

- Increasing your blinding rate–a clear sign of anxiety, Several people start blinking their eyes very quickly when they get excited (in combination with a faster heart rate). Since most people try to make contact with their pupils, it becomes obvious to others instantly. When you're anxious, be mindful of your blinking patterns, particularly when someone stares at you from close proximity.

- Slouching your head–indicates low self-esteem. People associate with strong self-confidence perked-up shoulders. Pull back your shoulders all the time. You will not only look more confident, but you will also feel more confident.
- Standing with Your Hands Crossed Over your Genitals –This casual posture almost guarantees you will lose some respect before you even have the opportunity to speak a single word. People who feel anxious or uncertain of themselves will take a defensive posture unconsciously. We also take a stance that covers one of their most vulnerable areas, their genitals. This posture forces down your arms and makes your whole body look smaller and weaker. Try to keep your palms on your sides and back on your feet.
- Strengthening your back with your hands–"I get tired! "Don't hold your head during a conversation with your elbows and wrists. Place your hands on the table and sit in front of you.
- Wipe your clothing with sweaty hands–a form of frenzied nervousness. When you wet your palms, just let them drip. Take some deep breaths and try calming.

- Sitting on your chair's edge Is a clear indication that you are mentally and physically distressed, It's a terrifying mentality that will also make others around you feel uncomfortable. Keep your back end squarely on the seat board. Use your back without raising your butt while bending forward.
- The tapping of the foot and thumbnail–usually indicates pain, impatience or boredom. Track and exercise your activities to keep your body at ease.
- Using Your Hands to Fidget with Small Things–a pad, a paper clip, etc It can also be interpreted as being unprepared. When you are in the company of others, it is always best to keep your hands at rest comfortably.
- Shifting body weight from foot to foot regularly– this is another move that usually indicates mental and physical pain. Others may also see this and presume you're willing to give up the discussion, particularly if you don't answer it explicitly. Do not move your feet every 2 or 3 minutes more than once.

HOW TO PAY ATTENTION TO YOUR OWN BODY LANGUAGE

Body language refers to the non-verbal cues that we use to communicate. According to researchers, these non-verbal cues make up a large part of daily communication. Through our facial expressions to our body movements, items we don't say can still communicate quantities of information.

It has been proposed that body language may account for between 60% and 65% of all communication.

Learning body language is crucial, but it is also vital to pay attention to other signals, such as meaning. In many situations, you should be looking at the signs as a collective rather than relying on a single action.

Be on the lookout for these factors when you're trying to interpret body language.

Facial expressions: let's face it, imagine how much a person can communicate with just a facial expression. A smile can signify acceptance or satisfaction. A frown can indicate rejection or unhappiness. In some situations, our facial expressions can show our true feelings about a specific situation. Although you say you feel fine, the look on your face can tell people differently.

Only a few examples of feelings that can be conveyed by facial expressions include:

- Joy

- Sadness

- Rage

- Shock

- Anxiety

- Confusion

- Excitement

- Hunger

- Contempt

The look on a person's face can even help to determine if we trust or believe what the individual says. One study found that the most accurate facial expression included a slight increase in eyebrows and a minimal smile. The expression holds both friendliness and trust.

Facial expressions are also among the most common modes of body language. The words used to communicate terror, rage, sorrow, and joy are common all over the world.

The research of a number of facial expressions related to different feelings, including happiness, rage, anxiety, shock, and sadness.

Research also indicates that we make judgments about people's intelligence based on their faces and expressions. One study found that people with smaller faces and more pronounced noses were more likely to be perceived as intelligent. Those with a smiling, happy smile were also found to be more intellectual than those with angry expressions.

Eyes: The eyes are often referred to as "soul windows" because they are capable of disclosing much about what a person feels or believes. When you engage in conversation with another person, taking notice of eye movements is a normal and important part of the contact process. Many common things you can find include whether people are making direct eye contact or averting their eyes, how much they are blinking, or whether their pupils are dilated.

While evaluating body language, pay attention to the following eye signals:

• Eye vision: when a person looks straight into your eyes when having a conversation, it means that they are listening and paying attention. Nevertheless, sustained eye contact may be dangerous. On the other hand, avoiding eye contact and often looking away may mean that a person is upset, embarrassed, or trying to hide his or her true feelings.

• Blinking: Blinking is normal, but you should also pay attention to whether a person is blinking too much or too little. People also blink harder when they feel upset or anxious. Infrequent blinking may mean that a person intentionally tries to regulate his or her eye movements.

•For example, a poker player may blink less often because he or she is purposely trying to appear unexcited about the hand he or she has played with.

• Pupil scale: The pupil size can be a very subtle non-verbal communication cue. Although light levels in the atmosphere influence pupil dilation, often feelings may also cause small differences in pupil size.

For example, you might have heard the phrase "bedroom eyes" used to describe someone's look when they're drawn to someone else. Highly dilated pupils, for example, may suggest that a person is fascinated or even aroused.

Mouth: Mouth gestures and motions may also be important for reading body language. For example, chewing on the bottom lip can signify an individual's feeling of anxiety, apprehension, or insecurity.

Covering your mouth may be an intention to be discreet if you are yawning or crying, this may be to hide an expression of disdain. Smiling is perhaps one of the strongest indicators of body language, but smiles can also be perceived in many respects. A smile may be genuine, or may be used to express false happiness, sarcasm, or even cynicism.

When assessing body language, pay attention to the following signs of mouth and

Lip:

• Pursed lips: tightening the lips may be a sign of discontent, disapproval, or distrust.

• Lipstick biting: people often pinch their lips when they are nervous, upset, or depressed.

• Covering the mouth: if people want to mask their emotional reactions, they may cover their mouths to avoid laughing or smiling.

• Up or down: Slight changes in the mouth are also subtle signs of human perception. When you raise your mouth slightly, it may mean that the person is feeling happy or hopeful. On the other hand, turning your mouth slightly down can be a sign of disappointment, rejection, or pure frowning.

Gestures: Gestures may be some of the most direct and obvious body language cues. Waving, nodding, and using the fingertips to signify numerical numbers are all very common and easy to understand. Nevertheless, certain movements may be cultural, and offering a thumb-up or a peace sign in another world might have a completely different meaning than in the United States.

The following examples are just a few typical movements and their potential meanings: • A clenched fist can signify frustration in some cases or unity in others.

• The thumbs up and down are often used as gestures of acceptance and disapproval.

• The 'Alright' symbol, made by rubbing the thumb and index finger together in a circle while spreading the remaining fingers, may be used to signify 'Good' or 'All Right.' In some parts of Europe, though, the same expression is used to show that you are sorry. In some countries in South America, the symbol is considered a lewd expression.

• The V symbol, created by raising the index and middle finger and dividing them to create a V-shape, means peace or triumph in some countries. In the United Kingdom and Australia, the sign has an unpleasant significance when the back of the hand is pointing outward.

Arms and legs Arms and legs may also be useful for conveying non-verbal knowledge. Crossing the weapons can suggest defensiveness. Crossing the legs away from another person can suggest irritation or dissatisfaction with that individual.

Some overt gestures, such as broadening your shoulders, may be an attempt to appear bigger or more dominant when holding your arms close to your chest, but may be an intention to diminish yourself or withhold your focus.

When evaluating body language, pay attention to some of the following signs that the arms and legs can convey:

• Crossed arms may mean that a person feels defensive, self-protective or closed.

• Holding hands on the shoulders may imply that a person is relaxed and in charge, or may also be a symbol of aggressiveness.

• Clinging your hands behind your back may indicate that a person feels bored, anxious, or even angry.

• Quickly clicking fingers or fidgeting can be an indication that a person is tired, anxious, or irritated.

• Crossed legs that mean that a person feels closed or in need of privacy.

The way we carry our bodies may be vital in the body's language. The term pose refers to the way in which we carry our bodies, as well as the overall physical structure of the person.

Posture can communicate a wealth of information about how a person feels, as well as clues about personality modalities, like whether someone is relaxed, responsive, or submissive.

Sitting up straight, for example, may mean that a person is concentrated and paying attention to what's going on. Sitting with a body hunched forward, on the other hand, can mean that the person is bored or indifferent.

When you're trying to read body language, consider recognizing some of the messages that a person's attitude can convey.

• Open stance involves keeping the body trunk open and uncovered. This style of pose demonstrates friendliness, transparency, and willingness.

• Closed stance entails covering the body's spine often by hunching forward and having the arms and legs crossed. This style of stance can be an indication of aggression, irritation, and anxiety.

Private Space Have you ever heard anyone refer to their need for personal space? Have you ever started to feel awkward when someone is just a little too close to you?

The term proxemics refers to the space between individuals when they communicate with each other. In as much as body movements and facial expressions can convey a lot of non-verbal details, so can this physical space between individuals.

The degree of social distance that exists in different situations:

• Intimate distance—6 to 18 inches: this level of physical distance often implies a closer relationship or greater comfort between people. This usually happens during intimate contacts, such as kissing, whispering, or touching.

• Personal distance—1.5 to 4 feet: the physical distance at this level usually happens between family members or close friends. The closer people can easily stand when engaging can be an indication of the level of intimacy of their relationship.

• Physical distance—4 to 12 feet: this amount of physical distance is often used by friends. With someone you know quite well, such as a co-worker you see several days a week, you may feel more comfortable talking at a closer distance. For situations where you don't know the other person well, such as a postal delivery driver you see only once a month, a distance of 10 to 12 feet might feel more comfortable.

• Social distance—12 to 25 feet: physical space at this point is commonly used in public speaking circumstances. Talking to a lot of students or making a career presentation are good examples of such scenarios.

Be aware of the degree of personal space that individuals need to feel comfortable will differ from culture to culture. Another example of this is the difference between people from Latin cultures and people from North America.

Persons from Latin countries tend to feel more comfortable standing next to each other as they communicate, whereas persons from North America need more personal space.

HOW TO RECOGNIZE WHETHER SOMEONE IS LYING OR TELLING THE TRUTH

Lying and lying are human activities that are normal. Until recently, little actual research has been conducted into how often people lie. Several polls have shown that at least often, as many as 96% of people admit to lying.

A national study of 1,000 U.S. adults found that 60% of respondents claimed they were not lying at all. Alternatively, the researchers found that only 5 percent of all subjects told almost half of all lies. The study suggests that while prevalence rates can differ, a small group of very prolific liars are likely to exist.

The reality is that from time to time most people are lying. Some of these lies are small white lies designed to protect the interests of someone else ("No, that shirt doesn't make you look fat!"). Such lies may be much more egregious in other situations (like lying on a resume) or even malicious (covering a crime).

Lying can be difficult to detect people because detecting lies is surprisingly bad. For example, one study found that people could only accurately detect lying 54 percent of the time in a laboratory setting — not amazing given a 50% hit rate alone by accident.

Several experiments have shown that even qualified analysts are remarkably poor at determining whether someone is lying or telling the truth.

Clearly, it is difficult to discriminate and measure the behavioral differences between honest and lying individuals. Researchers have tried to find various ways to detect deception. While there may not be a simple, tell-tale sign that somebody is dishonest (like the nose of Pinocchio), some useful indicators have been found by researchers.

Nevertheless, recognizing a deception mostly comes down to one thing, like many things — trusting your intuition. By knowing what signs a lie might accurately detect, and by learning how to heed your own gut reactions, you may be better able to detect falsehoods.

Signs of Lying Red Flags That Someone may Be Lying Some of the potential red flags identified by researchers that might indicate that people are misleading to include:• Being vague; offering few details• Repeating questions before answering them• Speaking in phrase fragments • Failure to provide specific details when a story is challenged • Grooming behaviors such as hair playing or pressing

When it comes to detecting lies, people often focus on "telling" the body language, or subtle physical and behavioral signs that reveal deception. Although body language signals can sometimes lead to deceit, research suggests that lying is not strongly associated with many of the more predicted behaviors.

Researcher Howard Ehrlichman, a psychologist who since the 1970s has been studying eye movements, found that eye movements do not mean lying at all. In reality, he implies that shifting eyes means that a person thinks, or more specifically, that they have access to their long-term memory.

Many experiments have shown that while human signs and actions are helpful markers of deceit, others are among the worst predictors that are most often correlated with lies (such as eye movements). Although body language can be a useful tool in the identification of lies, the key is to understand what signs should be taken into consideration.

Based On the Right Signals One meta-analysis found that while people still rely on reliable indicators to spot deceit, the issue could be the vulnerability of these indicators as measures of manipulation in the first place.

Some of the most common indicators of deceit that people pay attention to include:• Being vague: If the speaker seems to leave out important details deliberately, it may be because they lie.

• Vocal uncertainty: the individual is more likely to be perceived as dishonest if he seems confused or nervous.

• Indifference: shrugging, lack of expression, and bored posture may be signs of lying as the person attempts to avoid emotional conveyance and tells.

• Overthinking: If the individual seems to think too hard to fill in the story's details, it may be because they mislead you.

The lesson here is that while body language may be helpful, the right signals need to be taken into account. Experts suggest that using these symbols too heavily can hinder the ability to detect lies.

Ask them to tell Their story is often seen as a passive mechanism in the identification of reverse lie. People often assume that they can just analyze the body language and facial expressions of the alleged liar to find apparent "tells." While work has shown that this is a pretty bad way to detect lies, better results can be obtained by taking a more active approach to detecting lies.

Research suggests that it can improve the accuracy of lie identification by telling people to report their stories in reverse order rather than chronological order. As the cognitive load grows, verbal and non-verbal signals that differentiate between lying and telling the truth may become more evident.

Not only is it more cognitively taxing to tell a lie, but liars also expend much more mental energy to track their actions and assess others ' reactions. We are worried about their reputation to feel that their claims are heard by other people. All this takes considerable time, so if you throw yourself into a challenging task (like relaying their story in reverse order), narrative gaps and behavioural' tells' may become easier to spot.

For one report, 80 participants of mock were either telling the truth or lying about an incident being staged. Some of the people were asked in reverse order to report their experiences while others were actually telling their stories in chronological order. The researchers found that more behavioral clues to deception were revealed by the reverse order interviews.

55 police officers watched taped recordings from the first trial in a second experiment and were asked to decide who was lying and who was not. The investigation revealed that in the reverse order interviews law enforcement officers were better at detecting lies than in the chronological interviews.

Trust Your Instincts According to the findings of one report, your instant intestinal responses may be more effective than any deliberate identification of lie that you may attempt. Researchers in the study had 72 participants watching videos of interviews with suspects of the mock crime. Some of these offenders had stolen a $100 bill from a bookshelf while others had not, yet they were told to tell the investigator they hadn't taken the money.

Similar to previous studies, the participants were quite bad at detecting lies, with only 43 percent of the time accurately identifying the liars and 48 percent of the time the truth-tellers.

But the researchers also used implicit time tests for behavioral reaction to assess the more automatic and unconscious responses of the participants to the suspects. What they found was that the questions were more likely to involve words like "dishonest" and "deceitful" unintentionally with the perpetrators who were simply lying. They were also more likely to associate with the truth-tellers overtly terms like "true" and "honest."

So if our gut reactions are more reliable, why isn't it better for people to recognize dishonesty? Their unconscious connections may be impaired by intentional responses. Instead of focusing on our intuition, people focus on the conventional habits they often equate with deception including fidgeting and lack of contact with the eyes. Highlighting patterns that unreliably forecast deceptions makes distinguishing between truth and lies more challenging.

CHAPTER 6

MOST EFFECTIVE MIND CONTROL TECHNIQUES TIPS IN NLP

A fascinating form of destructive power that still exists in society is the techniques that control other minds. When perceiving the actions of the outside world, the mind is more sensitive.

Our mind consumes all the information that is needed and processes it. Our subconscious mind processes these results. Mostly the brain processes these pieces of information. We are consciously aware of only a few of the 1000s of information we perceive through our five senses.

Then, depending on certain circumstances, this screening, Therefore, this made it more susceptible to those forces where NLP is an effective tool for controlling the thinking of an individual.

The methods of mind control can affect one's behavior as these steps are the product of the previously controlled thoughts in your head. These approaches are based on Neuro-Linguistic Programming (NLP), which is capable of controlling the minds of people with well-equipped techniques and habits.

Here are the NLP's top few mind control techniques used to control other minds by skilled professionals.

1. Paying close attention to the person: experts pay close attention to a person's symptoms, such as eye movements, dilation of the eyes, nervous tics, body blush, body language, breathing rhythm, etc. They can infer a person's state of mind because a person's instant emotion is associated with such indications.

Such eye movements can be observed in order to determine how the information is perceived and interpreted. For example, if one of the participants was questioned about his car's color and he replied with his eyes going up to the right corner, then his response is produced visually.

Similarly, if the eyes are shifted left-top of the intersection, it will be tactile recollection as it recalls the car's light. Recent studies have shown it to be less accurate because it contains other variables that confuse it a little bit.

2. Speaking with a Human Brain Suggestive Frequency: Delivering words similar to the beats of the human heart, i.e. 45 to 72 beats per minute, which could cause a higher state of suggestibility to the brain.

3. Bypassing the conscious Mind by Voice Roll: This method is the voice roll phase-a patterned paced style that enshrines the desired point and thus bypasses the conscious mind to the person's subconscious mind. This is achieved by illustrating a monotonous patterned form of the desired phrase.

4. Secretly Making the Document Easily: Experienced NLP experts use violent vocabulary to improve suggestibility. The interaction with you will be built by closely examining you, making you more open to their

feedback by claiming to be your body language in a subtle form.

5. Creating Anchor and Sublimely Programming the Mind: This is the process of creating an anchor in you, making it easy to place you in a certain state just by pressing or manipulating and programming your mind sublimely.

5. Effective Way of Using the Hot Words: NLP practitioners use a specific word style that seems natural but is more subtle and permissive. Less descriptive are the hot terms that are more related to the senses. Terms like hearing that see that, feel free, ultimately means, now, then, if, etc. may immediately evoke a certain state of mind like thinking, witnessing, dreaming, and trigger the desired experience in mind as well. We also use some vague words to keep your thoughts under the track.

7. A Simple Inter-spiral Subconscious Brain Programming: In the subconscious mind of the subject, by the inter-spiral method, that is by dictating one thing while planting something else.

HOW KNOWING CBT CAN IMPROVE YOUR COMPREHENSION OF NLP

NLP is a study of subjective experience, studying how language and cognition affect our behavior. In NLP, you will learn how to filter the information you receive to understand its meaning, and how to communicate and act based on its interpretation.

For example, the generalization that all foreigners lighten Indians can adversely affect their relationship with working European bosses.

Communication that changes perceptions, sees and hears what is true "what", and increases productivity helps to overcome what appears to be preventing us from achieving what we want. Many coaches and corporate leaders use NLP today, and NLP is available to anyone who wants to set and achieve goals.

CBT, on the other hand, is primarily developed as a therapeutic technique that allows people to understand how thinking triggers the behavior and affects how they feel.

CBT is used primarily in the therapeutic context to help people reprogram their thinking patterns. For example, learn many rules because children need to update as they gain experience. Otherwise, they will start to have problems as adults.

For example, you may have noticed that your father was so strict that you should stay away from an authoritative person. But doing the same thing with your boss at work may not be the best for you today.

1. CBT involves a cognitive process that requires input about situations and behaviors that individuals are trying to change by changing their thoughts, beliefs, and attitudes. On the other hand, NLP techniques are not content dependent. That is, specific details about the situation or behavior may not be required.

2. NLP also helps models how the mind adds meaning to the data it receives through our senses.

3. Both NLP and CBT help people overcome limiting beliefs and move towards a more ecological way of life.

4. Although CBT can be used to identify and challenge limiting beliefs as they arise, NLP provides a framework to restructure them into something more realistic and useful. You. Because the NLP change process is based on hypnosis, it is important to understand and learn about hypnosis and help clients efficiently and effectively.

HOW TO CONTROL YOUR OWN DEEPEST THOUGHTS

You must recognize that you are currently at the mercy of several unwanted "squatters" living in your mind before you can become the master of your mind, and they are in charge of your thoughts. If you want to be their manager, you need to know who they are and what their purpose is, and then you can take responsibility and drive them out.

Here are four of your head's "squatters" producing the most dangerous and unproductive thoughts: 1. The Internal Critic This is your relentless critic, often a conglomeration of: • Comments from other people; your parents at times.

• Thoughts you generated on the basis of aspirations of your own or other peoples.

• Competition with others, including those in the newspapers.

• As a result of painful experiences such as betrayal and rejection, things you have told yourself. Your interpretation creates your self-doubt and self-blame, which in cases of rejection and betrayal are most likely undeserved.

The Inner Critic is motivated by pain, low self-esteem, lack of acceptance of self, and lack of self-love.

Why else would you be violated by that person? And since this person is you, why else would you be abusing yourself? Why are you going to let someone treat you badly?

2. The Worrier This person lives in the future; in the "what ifs" universe. The Worrier is motivated by fear that is often unfounded and has no reason for it. This person is sometimes motivated by fear that what happened in the past could happen again.

3. The reactor or troubleshooting maker This is the one that causes anger, frustration and pain. These triggers are the result of past unhealed wounds. It will be set off by any experience that is even closely related to a past wound.

This person can be set off with words or feelings, and sounds and smells can even set off.

The reactor has no real motivation and poor impulse control and is run by programming in the past that, if ever, no longer serves you.

4. The Sleep Depriver This can be a mix of numerous squatters including the inner strategist, the rehashed, and the ruminator, together with the inner critic and the worrier.

The inspiration of the Sleep Depriver may be:• As a response to the isolation he battles against• Taking care of the company you ignored during the day• Self-doubt, low self-esteem, fear and widespread anxiety • As mentioned above, how can you manage these squatters?

You are the thinker and observer of your thoughts as to how to master your mind. You have to pay attention to your thoughts in order to identify "who" is running the show; this will determine the technique you want to use.

Start every day with the intention to pay attention to your emotions and stop yourself while you hear of unwanted thoughts.

There are two ways of controlling your thoughts: • Method A–disrupt and erase them • Strategy B – completely eliminate them The second option is what is known as peace of mind!

The disruption and substitution strategy is a way to reprogram the subconscious mind. In the appropriate circumstances, the substitution thoughts will gradually become the "go to" thoughts.

Use the External Critic and Worrier Method A; and the Reactor and Sleep Depriver Technique B.

For the Inner Critic If you say something derogatory about yourself (calling yourself names, disrespecting yourself, or berating yourself), stop that.

You should scream "Wait!" (in your mind). Yes! No! No!"And, that's enough! Instead, if your negative thinking was about yourself, substitute it with an alternative or counter-thought or an assertion that starts with "I am." For instance, if your thought is, "I am such a failure," you should replace it with, "I am the Divine Creator of the Holy Spirit. I am a perfect spiritual being that learns to master the experience of man. I am an energetic, light, and material being. I'm beautiful, brilliant and beautiful. You can also have a conversation with yourself with the intention of discrediting the' word' that produced the idea, because you know whose voice it is:' Just because so - and-so said I was a loser doesn't make it true. It was his view, not a factual statement.

Or maybe they've been kidding because I took it seriously because I'm nervous. "When you know that you've got frequent self-critical thoughts, you should compose and pre-planning your alternative feelings by statements so you can be primed. This is the first squatter you ought to expel, if possible forcefully:• The Worrier rile up.

• The names you call yourself cause when others call those names, so it also maintains the Reactor's influence.

• If you want to fall asleep, they are often there so that he perpetuates the Sleep Depriver.

• They are aggressive and violent both verbally and emotionally.

• They're the self-esteem killer. They convince you not to be deserving. You're a fake! Get them out in the interests of your self-worth!

Eliminate the biggest enemy and the influence of the other three squatters will also be reduced.

Replace them with your best new friends helping, promoting and improving your life. This is a feeling in your subconscious that you want.

Long-term anxiety for the Worrier is psychologically, socially and physically dangerous. It may have long-term consequences for wellbeing.

Anxiety initiates the reaction to fight or flight, creates anxiety in mind and anxiety in the body.

You should be able to detect a "worried mind" from your intuition immediately. The physiological signs that fear's battle or flight reaction has kicked in are: • Increased heart rate, blood pressure, or adrenaline rush • Shallow breathing or breathlessness• Muscle tension Use the above approach to stop and then remove any anxiety feeling. But this time you're going to replace your anxiety feelings with happy thoughts for the result you seek.

This is the time to engage with it if you believe in a higher power. Here's an example: Instead of thinking for my loved ones flying in poor weather, I'm doing the following (I consider it a prayer): "Thank you so much for watching over.

Thank you for watching and keeping your car clean, roadworthy and maintenance-free without warning. Thank you for only having safe, diligent and warning drivers around him / her. So thank you for keeping him / her secure, attentive, so aware. "Smile as you talk about it or speak it aloud, and word it in the present tense; both will help you feel it and maybe even begin to believe it.

If you are able to visualize what you are hoping for, the vision will intensify the sensation and maximize the effect on your vibrational area.

Now take a soothing breath, through your nose slowly, and through your mouth slowly. Bring as many men as you like!

Replacing negative feelings with joy will diminish reactive actions by removing the steam from the reactor.

For example: if your child gets lost in the store, screaming at them is the usual parental response that accompanies the frightened thinking.

"I told you never to leave my sight." In the first place, this reaction adds to the level of fear of the child. It also tells them that when he or she makes a mistake, mom and/or dad will get angry, which may lead them to lie to you or not tell you things in the future.

When they arise, change the scary thoughts: "Thank You (your Higher Power choice) for watching over my child and keeping him safe. Thank you for helping me find him early. "So, after this thought process, when you see your boy, joy will be your only response, and that seems like a better alternative for all involved people.

For the Trouble-Maker, Reactor or Over-Reactor Permanently removing this squatter can require a little more time and contemplation after the fact to locate and repair the causes of the triggers; but until then, you will keep the Reactor from getting out of control by inducing deliberate breathing as soon as you notice its existence.

The thoughts or emotions of the Reactor trigger the reaction to the fight or flight just as with the Worrier. His presence's biochemical signs will be the same. You should be able to tell the difference between fear, indignation, irritation, or discomfort with a little attention: • Increased heart rate and blood pressure; rush in Shallow adrenaline breathing or breathlessness • Muscle tension I'm sure you've heard the idea of counting to ten when you get frustrated— well, you can make those ten seconds much more effective if you breathe during actively.

Conscious breathing is as simple as it sounds; be mindful of your breathing. Pay attention to the air that goes in and out.

Use your nose to breathe in: • Feel the air in your nostrils.

Experience overflowing and widening the lungs

• Focus on can your heart.

Exhale through your nose:• Feel emptying your lungs.

• Keep on dropping your butt.

• Notice the air coming out of your nostrils.

Do this as much as you want. If you want, leave the situation. It provides the time for normalizing the adrenaline.

Instead, with a calmer, more rational perspective, you will address the situation and prevent harmful behavior.

One of the problems caused by this squatter is that it leads to the concerns of sleep depriver. You will decrease reactive actions by evicting or at least regulating the engine, which will decrease the need for rehashing and ruminating that may keep you from sleeping.

Control your mind to save you and your relationships from putting stress on the Reactor!

I was afflicted by a very common problem for the Sleep Depriver (they are made up of the Inner Planner, the

Rehashes and the Ruminator, along with the External Critic and the Worrier): I couldn't shut my mind off at bedtime. This weakness stopped me from dreaming and thus getting to sleep

SECRETS TO CONTROL YOUR LANGUAGE

Our bodies have their own language, and their words are not always kind. Your body language is likely to be an integral part of who you are, up to the point where you may not even think about it.

The following are the 15 most common body language failures people make and emotionally intelligent people are careful to avoid.

1. Slouching is a sign of disrespect. It tells you that you are bored and do not want to be where you are now. I'll never tell my boss, "I don't understand why I have to listen to you," but if you lean forward, you don't have to do it.

The brain is wired to equate power with the number of space people occupy. The power position is to stand straight with your shoulders behind. Maximize the space to fill. On the other hand, slouching is the result of folding the form. It occupies less space and consumes less power.

Maintaining the right attitude respects and promotes engagement from both ends of the conversation.

2. Exaggerated gestures imply that you are extending the truth. Show leadership and self-confidence with small, controlled gestures, aim for open gestures (spread your arms, show your palms, etc.) and tell them that you have nothing to hide.

3. Looking at the clock while talking to someone is a clear sign of rudeness, impatience, and ego swelling. It sends you a message that you have more to do than talking to the people you are with and you are eager to leave them.

4. If you keep yourself away from others and do not lean on conversations, you describe yourself as uninteresting, uninteresting, uncomfortable, and possibly even distrustful.

Try leaning towards the person who is talking and tilt your head a little while listening to them. This shows who speaks that you have full focus and attention.

5. Crossing arms or legs is a physical barrier, suggesting that you are not open to what others are saying. Even if you're smiling or having a good conversation, your opponent may have a persistent feeling that you're keeping yourself locked out.

Even if you feel comfortable breaking your arms, if you want people to be open-minded and interested in what they are saying, resist the urge to do so.

6. Due to the disagreement between words and facial expressions, people start to feel that something is incorrect and suspect that you are trying to deceive them.

For example, a nervous smile when rejecting an offer during negotiations will not help you get what you want. You only feel anxious about others working with you.

7. Exaggerated nods indicate anxiety about approval. People may recognize your nod as an attempt to show that you do not actually agree or understand that you are not.

8. Tweaking and fixing hair can mean anxiety, excessive energy, self-consciousness and distraction. People feel

that you are overly concerned with your physical appearance and not fully interested in your career.

9. Avoid eye contact, and there appears to be something hidden that raises doubt. Also, the lack of eye contact may indicate a lack of confidence and interest that you never want to convey in a business environment.

When you look down when you are speaking, you appear to be lacking in self-confidence or self-aware and have lost the effect of words. Keeping your eyes level is especially important when creating complex or important points.

On the other hand, persistent eye contact conveys confidence, leadership, strength, and intelligence. It is possible to engage without direct, constant eye contact, but complete negligence obviously has a negative impact on your professional relationship.

10. Eye contact that is too strong may be perceived as offensive or an attempt to dominate. Americans maintain eye contact for an average of 7 to 10 seconds. Listening is longer than talking. How to disconnect a

contact also sends a message. Glancing down conveys the submission, confident looking at the side.

11. Rolling your eyes is a sure way to signal a lack of respect. Fortunately, it may be a habit, but it is optional. You can control it and it is worth the effort.

12. If you grimace or generally expresses unhappy, no matter what your mood, people around you will get a message that they are angry. Feeling as though they were judged, Skull diverts people.

But a smile suggests that you are open, reliable, confident, and friendly. MRI studies have shown that the human brain responds favorably to smiling people, leaving a lasting positive impression.

13. A weak handshake indicates a lack of authority and confidence, while a too strong handshake

14. Smiling helps create a sense of pride while keeping you comfortable and reducing your stress levels. Not only does it slow down your heart rate, but it also releases endorphins that can combat the body's stress hormones. Smiling can also be helpful during an interview or a presentation, as it will help you calm and comfort other people in the room.

15. Be mindful of your stance It is important for confident body language to have good posture.

In order to portray yourself as a more confident person, composure is necessary. Try to keep your back straight against the chair as you sit down and your feet flat on the cement. Obviously, the legs should be bent at the right angle. Make sure that your hands are down and your head is lifted as you give a message from a standing position. You can find yourself idle or aloof while you slouch. If you're seated on the chair's bottom, you might seem too nervous or anxious.

16. Make sure your body language is always accessible and engaged in your body language. People should want to communicate with you, feel comfortable doing so, and feel like you're having a conversation or discussion with them. Engaging includes not only transparent body language, but also laughing, nodding, and imitating the gestures or actions of another so that they can know you are on the same emotional level. It can also mean standing up and sitting with them and getting closer to a hug when it's time to close the deal or end the conversation.

17. Be mindful of your arms and legs Almost everyone has felt the sensation of not knowing what to do with their arms and legs, and you can build awkward body language when you become aware of your posture and concentrate on it. Crossing your arms is a common problem because it allows you to see yourself as aggressive, self-protective or otherwise locked. Clutching your hands behind your back could make you look bored, nervous, or even angry. Holding them back together and before you can mean you're nervous.

You also need to watch how you cross your legs if you're sitting down. It is important that you cross your legs towards the other person if you feel more comfortable crossing your legs. Crossing your legs away from them may cause you to feel uncomfortable or dislike them. Crossing the ankles can be a gesture of holding back something from the conversation.

18. Practice a firm handshake: Nothing more than a firm, strong handshake shows confidence. It's also an indication that somebody needs to do business with you, and being right is a crucial factor. You want the handshake to be solid, but certainly not to the point where you break or in any way damage someone's

hand. Make sure your palms are dry and send up and down a few shakes while maintaining contact with your feet. A strong handshake, though exuding confidence, makes a good first impression.

19. Refrain from fidgeting: Grab your attention by making your presentation more interactive When you give a presentation, whether it's for a few or a few hundred people, make sure you avoid fidgeting. It shows not only a lack of faith, but also a lack of preparedness. It is possible to think of any kind of tense body language as fidgeting, so be mindful of what the body is doing. Things like tapping your foot, biting your nails, twisting your hair, or touching your face over and over again will give others the feeling you're not self-assured.

When you're making a presentation, fidgeting will make you feel nervous and unsure about the ideas you're presenting. Getting mindful of these patterns will give you better control of them.

20. Maintain proper eye contact: The contact with the eye is a sign of trust and trust. It can also reassure someone you're committed, happy, and open, and it can make it easier for people to communicate with you.

Although eye contact is extremely beneficial, it is also essential to maintain the appropriate amount. Too much contact with your eyes might make you look a bit violent. You can make people uncomfortable as it activates their sympathetic nervous system, putting them on the defense, once you pass the point from gazing to staring.

21. Track your facial expressions In order to avoid looking irritated or stoic, always be mindful of your facial expressions. Your face is the part of you that will attract the most scrutiny during a discussion, and you will be watched by a person to make sure you look at them, listen to them, and hear what they mean.

With our facial expressions, we can convey a tremendous range of emotions, so find out what expressions work best with your message. Feeling compassionate will help to show that what you are expressing is comfortable and confident.

22. Pay attention to your hands: The parts of your brain that are essential to the development of speech not only display movement when you sing, but also when you wave your hands. Movements are related to voice, so you can actually boost your thought process by adding

the movements into your speech delivery. You may also note a less sluggish voice and an increase in your verbal output. Terms like "yeah" and "oh" are also going to decrease. Find physical movements that can help clear your mind and work with your words well.

When engaging with others, you should always know what your hands do — and say — and make sure you don't accidentally make inappropriate movements with your hands or fingers. It can also sound rude to poke or stab a finger at someone's nose. Instead, do so with an open palm when you need to gesture during a discussion, bringing all your fingers together tightly. Open hands can communicate acceptance, openness, and cooperation with palms facing up.

STRATEGIES TO INFLUENCE AND MANIPULATE EVERYONE THANKS TO NLP

The worst mistake you can make when you ask anyone for anything is asking them to "think it over." Here's why: people have too much to worry about.

Their mind is already jammed between their work, their families, and their own interests and friends, like a bag on the edges. Add another sock, and it's going to explode.

We "forget" about things that aren't very important to them to stop it, or they don't think very hard because they care about you. It's not because they're stupid or lazy. They're just busy, and the priority list probably isn't very high.

So the best strategy is not to expect them to talk about it.

Do that for them.

• Instead of wanting them to see how your blog post would help their audience, clarify it, and offer examples of similar blogs that have been well done in the past • Instead of inviting someone to hold a webinar with you, set up your own webinar, landing pages, and contacts, and submit them as part of your presentation• Instead of convincing a client to write an essay from scratch, send them a dozen different posts. Explain your argument. Offer evidence. Ask them why and what to do next.

If you're doing it right, it's not going to feel like talking. It's going to be more like giving advice.

And they're going to say yes. Not because of the mystic powers of persuasion, but because of everything you've learned, and it's a no-brainer.

2. Launch an avalanche It's a lot like launching an avalanche to create a successful marketing campaign.

You climb the mountain first, and then you find the biggest boulder at the top, and then you sweat and cough and struggle to drive over the boulder, and then you sit down and watch peacefully as the boulder falls into other rocks, finally knocking down the entire side of the mountain.

The lesson?

The first major yes is a pain in the ass to get, but it's easy to get all the other yeses if you get it from the right person.

For example: • It's hard to get a famous blogger to share your message, but once they do, thousands or perhaps even hundreds of people can retweet them• Convincing a pioneer in your market to advertise your product is difficult, but once they do, everyone else will want to promote it too• Convincing a celebrity buyer to send you a testimonial can be challenging, but once you do it, sales increase and have furth

They're telling you to start and work your way up from the bottom because it's easier.

But it's just an illusion, really. Yeah, it's easier to push over a small rock than to push over a boulder, but the boulder is much more likely to cause an avalanche. So while getting top people to help you is more effort in the beginning, in the long run it's actually less work, and the outcomes are far, far better.

3. Ask for an inch, take a mile, you have heard the phrase, "Show them an inch, and they're going to take a mile," right?

It should be derogative. It's meant to be an appeasement alert. It's supposed to protect you from being abused.

But it's great, too.

Each time you ask for anything, never start asking up front for anything. Start small instead. Getting started is quick. Reduce risk when flopping. Let them see for themselves the effects.

Then call for more when all goes well. And more. And there's more.

You may think this is immoral, but if all goes well, why not press for more? It's not being exploited. It's a sense of common sense.

For example:• If you want to write a guest post for a popular blog, begin by pitching the idea in one or two words, then give them a diagram, and then write the full draft of the post • If you want to do a JV campaign with a pioneer in your industry, start by asking them to email your launch material to only 10% of their list, and then 50% of their list, and then 100% of their list. It's an intelligent business. No one likes to risk everything up front and your chances of getting them to say yes go through the roof by offering progressive levels of engagement.

4. Always have a clear deadline The keyword is "time." We've all had salesmen asking us, "Alright, you'd better get back to me soon, because I've got three more prospects arriving this afternoon, and I don't know how long it's going to last."

There are no customers, and no urgency exists. The salesman is so desperate that he is willing to lie, not only losing him the trust, but potentially also the bid.

And they're not just salesmen.

How many occasions have you been issued completely artificial deadlines by other people, thinking it's going to inspire you to act? Our teachers do it, our employers do it, our families do it, and you probably did it without knowing about it.

Don. Stop.

It's not only counterproductive, it's completely unnecessary. It's easy to create real urgency. You can build it into your everyday life with a little thought. For example: • Instead of forever leaving a free report on your blog, tell everyone that it's only going to be available for seven days, and then start charging $7 for it. Not only will you get a lot more downloads, but other bloggers will be much more likely to promote it in the window• Instead of allowing JV partners to dictate when they're going to promote your product, schedule a launch, announce it to your list, and then forward the announcement to partners, inviting them to participate•

Instead of asking customers for testimonials whenever they're there, show them up. You need it by then, or you can't include it Will some of them bow out, saying they're too busy right now, and they're going to catch you next time?

Of course, but it's better than never getting it all going. And if you let someone control schedules, that's just what's going to happen.

5. Give ten times as much as you're getting, you know you're supposed to give, right? But what you really don't know is how much to offer.

Most advertisers mistakenly assume that this is a ratio of 1:1.

You should provide a guide before you call for a connection. You should send a raise before calling for promotion. You should do one thing that merits a testimonial before you call for a testimony.

That's false, though. Great advertisers use a 10:1 scale, not just in practice, but in value: • If you want 100 guests, give them 1,000 • If you want $1,000 of product sales, then sell $10,000 in their goods• If you want one testimonial, do ten separate heroic acts of customer service deserving of a testimonial.

Yeah, it's a lot of work, but it's affecting the quality.

6. March for something bigger than you think on a street corner there are two homeless people.

The first man has a regular run-of - the-mill sign that says, "Spare a few dollars? On the other hand, the second guy has a much more peculiar sign: "It's not possible to feed my kids, and it's breaking me apart. Aid, please, so I can stop feeling like such a horrible parent. "Which one would you aid more? The other, right?

Forget to give him a couple of dollars. You would drive him to the grocery store with a sign like that and give him $200 worth in grocery stores. I think I'd do it.

That's the strength of being greater than yourself for something. It's taking care of people.

And it extends to everything: • Instead of writing yet another form of blogging, take a stand on an important issue, argue with both zeal and unassailable rationale• Instead of beginning another me-too consultancy company, create a movement, work tirelessly to improve your customers ' lives• Instead of selling yet another step-by-step book, sell a concept full of inspirational instances. Just for having the opportunity to help you spread the word, they feel grateful.

7. Do you want to know what distinguishes a great marketer from a bad one?

It's shameful.

I'm not referring to a lack of awareness, a gregarious, extroverted personality, or any other way we look at advertisers historically. These stereotypes are mostly myths.

No, by guilt, I mean this: an unshakable conviction that what you're doing is good for the world and determination to do anything to make it come into being.

You don't publish it and forget it when you believe in your work. You preach it day after day, week after week, month after month, year after year, working tirelessly to spread the message and fail to relax until they do.

155

You don't balk at sales if you believe in your company. You're reveling in it. Not because you are greedy or needy or arrogant, but because you know that your product is going to help them, it is your responsibility to get them to buy. No matter what it takes.

You don't beg for donations if you believe in your charity. You are calling for them. They are taking people by the hands and looking at them in the eyes and showing them what you are doing is changing the world, and it is time for them to step up and do their part.

It's not a question of money. It is not a question of prestige. It's not even a tradition.

It's about having to fall in love. It's about being happy. It's about seeing such a beautiful vision that you can't help but fight to make it real.

HOW NLP CAN BRING YOU TO INFLUENCE THE MASSES

Neuro Linguistic Programming gives us a variety of strategies to develop our perception, conversation and behavior.

NLP's roots come from the study and replication of clones–individuals who have been good at what they have achieved and then reproduce it to achieve similar results.

Our ability to understand what works is key to our success in business. There are seven of the observations or techniques to get you started here that we can replicate as managers to help us get even better at what we do.

1. Create a compelling vision to encourage others

We need to be transparent in our own heads where we want to go as a company and as a team before we can start leading others. We can't expect others to follow if we don't know.

2. Building a relationship to build a culture of confidence

Without a real connection with our team's individuals, we may be just a figurehead that our title tells people to follow. It's just enforcement and it's only going to get you so far. In order to really leverage the team's brain power and skills, we will engage with people as individuals.

3. Gain insight into how people think as people give us clues about what they think and how they think every day. NLP therapists listen to words closely, they track body language and behavior to help them understand what may happen. That and actually asking our colleagues gives us a real chance to get the best out of them.

3. Using cognitive positions to gain a fresh perspective
In particular in the customer care and hospitality sectors, placing oneself in the place of others is normal. This allows us to understand what the other person might be like. Through motivating us to look at things from other perspectives, visual positions help establish this notion. This may include the observer's or' fly on the wall,' which allows us to clearly see from an objective point of view all sides of the story.

5. Modeling others as a blueprint for success

A successful approach for administrators is to concentrate on what's effective for everyone and then learn how to do it. Like the pioneers of NLP, the sequence of events and what they mean at each point observe and question people who are good in a particular area. Real results can be obtained by creating a model of this process and then replicating it throughout the organization.

6. Access useful internal resources in challenging situations

An excellent coach knows that the coaches has the resources that they need to succeed most of the time. Helping the other person find them is the trick. Accessing previous achievements ' feelings, strengths and trust allow us to apply them in different situations.

7. Personal values also fuel the desire to consider the beliefs of other people. Knowing what is important in terms of their work for people can help us create an atmosphere in which they can thrive. If it is necessary for them to have the responsibility to carry out a mission without pressure from their boss, think about how you can allow them the room to do this.

NLP AND NEGOTIATION SKILLS
Good negotiating is not as challenging as it may seem at first. Good negotiating skills come down to reasoning

and strategy when you really break it down. Note, no one wants to have disagreements — if not handled with care, they are awkward and emotionally taxing.

Everyone has positive intentions, but it's easy to turn into an ugly pissing match in the wrong setting for a meeting. But often two very different things are getting what you want and winning a fight. And while "being right" or "proving the other person wrong" may sound good at the moment, achieving what you want needs a decision to be made between an "I told you so" short-term so long-term achievement.

Here are a professional negotiator's six most important rules:

1. Framing the conversation as a partnership to solve a common problem:
2. Expert bargaining tactics The most important thing to remember while negotiating is that the enemy is the issue itself— not the person right in front of you. When you follow an attitude of "me vs. them," your body language, word collection, and the sound that communicates them will unintentionally create a competitive environment. Yet agreements are not a winner-and-loser

situation— conversely, a win - win situation is supposed to be created.

Your first step will be to set your goals from the most immediate objective to the more general purpose(s).

"Stepping up": Stepping up means simply setting the larger goal within a smaller, more immediate desire or goal. If your goal is to drink the beer in your refrigerator, the bigger goal may be to get drunk— but it may also be to take something off your mind, or just relax.

Perhaps your spouse is telling you to attend tonight's yoga class, but you've been watching the game with your ears. You can learn by "stepping up" that the intention of your spouse is to relieve stress, in which case a long back-rub can be just as effective and allow you to watch the game simultaneously.

Using a great example where an employee is looking for a raise— although their core intention is not to make more money, but to raise their quality of life. In this situation, if an increase does not fit in the budget, the company has many other choices, such as expanding the vacation time or changing the workload of the employee to fit their workflow better.

In "stepping up"— establishing the more general purpose behind the action — new options are available, and where all sides leave happy, a successful agreement will proceed.

A major advantage of stepping up is to reassure each group that their purpose is not simply to win the target of a deal, but rather to accomplish a greater objective that they believe will help them succeed.

In fact, there is almost always a common goal that both sides share — although they get lost in the heat of the immediate conflict. If a meeting threatens to intensify into a dispute, standing up and setting the larger common goal becomes necessary to steady the dialogue.

3. No immediate response: Expert negotiator tactics
This is one of the most important skills to cultivate for successful negotiation: when someone is bringing forward their idea(s), do not, ever, present an instant counter argument, It takes courage to share your ideas,

and reacting quickly with an opposing view is a sure-fire way to put them on the defensive.

When someone makes a suggestion, it means they have a vested interest in seeing their proposals play out — consciously or subconsciously. Therefore, this is where almost 100 percent of their attention will be devoted immediately after making the proposal.

That's why this is the time when they'll be less open to your suggestions, and if you're trying to pipe in with your thoughts too soon, you could speak to thin air as well.

Rather, give the attention it deserves to their idea— ask questions and explore their proposal. It is not only more polite, but it will also leave them open for reciprocating and sharing the thoughts in depth. Ultimately, if you disagree, do not use the idea of saying the series.

You will be annoyed by flat telling "I disagree" and put up a wall that will keep them from listening to your argument. Alternatively, first, explain your position and your concerns. Or better yet, ask questions that will push them in their presentation to answer your issues and any possible gaps.

4. Asking questions: Asking questions can be an indispensable bargaining tool, which helps you to address the views of someone else with respect— but the focus here is on "respectfully."

It is important to maintain a partnership and, indeed, to avoid any sign of hostility in your voice before you ask a question. If you're asking questions with a sarcastic tone in your speech, you can guarantee that they're going to pull something out of their butt that might make no sense at all, or that they're not really behind them, but they're going to add intangible bricks to their case base.

Alternatively, the questions should apply to the cracks within these bricks in a calm manner. The right questions would encourage the opponent, instead of having to do it for them, to undermine their own case, which will only result in resentment.

When you ask a question, it is also useful to ask for permission. For instance, "Do you think I should ask you a question? "This will magnify the value of the question and, in turn, discourage them from dodging the answer.

5. Proposing a hypothetical situation: 4 expert negotiator tactics Proposing a hypothetical situation in which your proposal might be used is a simple way to lower a negotiation's defensive guard.

It subtly persuades the rival to step away from the negotiation ring and use their imagination to create a scenario in which they can really see from your point of view. It may be hypothetical, but it takes you one step closer to your bargaining side. If in the conversation you hit a wall, phrases such as, "under what conditions would you be willing to give up on this? "But this is just a basic-line expression, which is best adapted to your particular situation.

If you're trying to negotiate an increase, but your boss doesn't budget, there might be a good question "under what conditions would you be willing to raise me? "This will require the boss to determine the requirements you need to lift.

In a couple's earlier example, where one wants to spend the night doing yoga and the other wants to watch the game, the question could read, "under what conditions are you willing to go with me to yoga? "I'd go just about anytime as long as the game isn't on!" to which their spouse might reply. "Sixth. Beware of intimidation tactics: 5 expert negotiator strategies

Most people enjoy dealing with intimidation tactics and will use provocative words like "Really?" That's your point of view? "This is it? What are you going to do with that? "In order to make almost any argument sound stupid, certain types of phrases can be used. In this case, the worst thing you can do is try to provide further logic.

Doing so will make it look like you're not comfortable in your previous points, and will eventually replace what might have been a strong initial claim with flimsy new points you've just come up with on the spot, in all probability.

Rather, the best thing to do here is to stand firm in the role you've already claimed. Calmly use phrases like "Of course, that's my reasoning" or "Yup — that's the only reason I need." If someone explicitly challenges your reasoning rather than providing a reasonable counter argument, chances are they've resorted to grasping straws with loose questions designed to intimidate. Here the trick is to make it look stupid they even asked.

CONCLUSION

Have you ever clicked on someone when you saw them? If so, it was presumably because, verbally and nonverbally, the contact preferences aligned.

Obviously, we change our speaking style to suit the person with whom we are talking; it is called matching. Matching is an essential part of effective communication.

You suit somebody in different ways, like your breathing. If you breathe at the same pace as you do, you build a strong bond with another person.

When you do it softly, coordinated breathing is more effective, so don't go overboard. Basically, coordinating the posture should be an automatic activity such as walking or driving a vehicle through a common area.

Pacing and leading people can also be influenced. Apparently, people copy the body language of each other, so you can manipulate their actions if you have someone's attention. The author was at a programmed where the presenter took a deep breath at one point—and the action was repeated by nearly all the audience.

The communication style of a person often reveals a lot about their way of thinking. Most people are categorized as one of these groups, based on how they perceive.

To portray the universe and illustrate their emotions, certain people use visual imagery. Some use words like "It looks like" or "I see it." For interpretation and conversation, some rely more on their hands. They say things like "Everything sounds fine" or "Stop telling me..." Through their thoughts and physical sensations, the third group expresses and understands the universe.

They use phrases such as "I feel great" or "I don't grasp the idea." By matching them in their speaking style, you can strengthen your bond with someone. However, if you mismatch when they use auditory language, you will distance yourself from them by using visual language.

Have you ever heard of something frightening and felt anxious all of a sudden? Not unexpectedly, both physically and emotionally, the emotions have a significant impact on how you react.

The feelings are like pictures of a film reel, and the emotions can be profoundly changed. So, keeping to the same example, by changing the colors, brightness or noise level of the stimuli in your mind, you can change your feelings. Think of it like watching a movie in a theatre instead of at home: either way, it's the same movie, but the theater experience is stronger.

You can, therefore, choose to decrease your negative feelings or maximize your favorable feelings. But how is that?

Through anchoring it to another type of stimuli that you can control, you can enhance a sensation. For starters, think of a happy experience; it should be so lovely when you remember to smile. Imagine now that this experience is attached to a "fun" lever and pull the lever.

This might feel stupid, but you can imagine pulling it whenever you feel down and you come to associate the trigger with a happy feeling. Your brain remembers the feeling of happiness, and you will begin to feel better.

Anchoring can also be used to quench your fears. One of the writers had a client who could use anchoring to conquer his fear of women talking — having phobia to speak with them even when he had much interested in ski jumping, a sport where one ski off a mountain flying at high speeds from a ramp into the air.The author helped the guy to connect the feeling of anticipation to the women's talk experience. He felt at home with the other sex once he leveraged the happiness he had from ski-jumping.

You start controlling your life by controlling your mind. Most problems, such as stress, fear, anxiety, and lack of self-discipline, are rooted in your thinking. Start making positive changes in your life using neuro-linguistic programming guidelines. Your ideas are healthy–use them for your good!